PRAISE FOR
RUMORS OF GOD

Rumors is filled with the same forward-thinking spirit that defines its authors, Jon Tyson and Darren Whitehead. One thing is for certain, these guys love the Church, and the Christ who fashions it together through lives reborn by the unique and ageless grace He exudes. Their Gospel is classically timeless, but everything about the way they write, think, and lead feels fresh and future. If you'll let them, they'll gladly lead you there.

LOUIE GIGLIO

PASTOR, PASSION CITY CHURCH

Many church leaders can exegete the Bible, sadly few can exegete our culture. Tyson and Whitehead reveal their teaching gifts as they deftly accomplish while illuminating a vision for what our life with God can be. *Rumors of God* will be a convicting and encouraging read for Christians searching for more.

SKYE JETHANI

AUTHOR, *WITH: REIMAGINING THE WAY YOU RELATE TO GOD*

In a world that perpetually castigates the Christian Church for its many failures, Jon Tyson and Darren Whitehead give us hope. With wisdom beyond their years, these next generation leaders shift our collective gazes from the Church's blemishes to her beauty, from her prominent failures to her promising future. Both challenging and encouraging, *Rumors of God* will reintroduce you to a God worth talking about.

GABE LYONS

AUTHOR, *THE NEXT CHRISTIANS*, FOUNDER, Q,

COAUTHOR, *UnCHRISTIAN*

Jon Tyson and Darren Whitehead are two emerging voices that bring a fresh perspective to today's leadership landscape. More than just critics or theorists, they are modeling what they write about in compelling and practical ways. In *Rumors of God* they depict a vision of the church that's hopeful, inspiring and worth giving your life to. Highly recommended!

BRAD LOMENICK

EXECUTIVE DIRECTOR, *CATALYST*

Jon and Darren are hopeful practitioners of the kind of discipleship that overflows with spiritual verve and apostolic vision. For those who are jaded by the church, or have become cynical about the power of the Gospel in our time, *Rumors of God* is a great antidote. A worthy read.

ALAN HIRSCH

AUTHOR, DREAMER, ACTIVIST

(WWW.THEFORGOTTENWAYS.ORG)

Darren and Jon invite us into a hopeful, exciting way of looking at both the world and the church. I was captured by their stories of what's happening all around us and also their dreams of what could be. I have little interest in reading an account of what's wrong with the world or what's wrong with the church, but in this book, I've been inspired and energized by what's right in both. With passion and wisdom, Darren and Jon are guiding us to a better future.

SHAUNA NIEQUIST
AUTHOR, *COLD TANGERINES* AND *BITTERSWEET*

Rumors of God is part of a growing rebellion that believe the church is not dead but actually more alive than ever! In *Rumors*, Jon and Darren freshly remind us of Jesus' magnificent beauty and the raw, organic truths that give all of us life.

DAVE GIBBONS
ACTIVIST AND AUTHOR, *XEALOTS: DEFYING THE GRAVITY OF NORMALITY* (XEALOT.NET AND NEWSONG.NET)

If you look around you, if you listen to more than the sound, and if you probe below the surface there are rumors of God everywhere. Once you begin to hear the rumors, all of life changes and we begin to fix on the kingdom dreams of Jesus. This book invites us to find the rumors of God all around us. Read it, but be ready to be changed because you will also begin to hear the rumors.

SCOT MCKNIGHT
AUTHOR, *ONE.LIFE: JESUS CALLS,
WE FOLLOW* AND *JESUS CREED FOR STUDENTS*

Each time I have had the opportunity to hear Darren teach, I have gone away moved and inspired. Now, in *Rumors of God*, he and Jon do that again. They remind us that God is still here, and still very much able to be found.

Dr. Henry Cloud
author, *Necessary Endings*

The rumors are true. God is moving. He is alive. Closer than ever. And that truth should radically impact our lives and outlook. Darren and Jon deliver an inspiring and practical guide to having a passionate relationship with the God that you always heard about, but weren't sure was real or just a fairytale.

Mike Foster
People of the Second Chance,
author, *Gracenomics*

RUMORS OF GOD

DARREN WHITEHEAD & JON TYSON

RUMORS OF GOD

EXPERIENCE THE KIND OF FAITH YOU'VE ONLY HEARD ABOUT

THOMAS NELSON
Since 1798

NASHVILLE   DALLAS   MEXICO CITY   RIO DE JANEIRO

Published in Nashville, Tennessee, by Thomas Nelson. Thomas Nelson is a registered trademark of Thomas Nelson, Inc.

Thomas Nelson, Inc., titles may be purchased in bulk for educational, business, fundraising, or sales promotional use. For information, please e-mail SpecialMarkets@ ThomasNelson.com.

Scripture quotations marked TNIV are taken from the Holy Bible. TODAY'S NEW INTERNATIONAL VERSION®. Copyright © 2001, 2005 by Biblica, Inc.™ Used by permission of Zondervan. All rights reserved worldwide. www.zondervan.com

Scripture quotations marked KJV are from the King James or Authorized Version of the Bible.

Scripture quotations marked NKJV are from THE NEW KING JAMES VERSION. © 1982 by Thomas Nelson, Inc. Used by permission. All rights reserved.

Scripture quotations marked NIV are taken from the Holy Bible. NEW INTERNATIONAL VERSION®. Copyright © 1973, 1978, 1984, 2011 by Biblica, Inc.™ Used by permission of Zondervan. All rights reserved worldwide. www.zondervan.com

Scripture quotations marked NLT are from Holy Bible, New Living Translation. © 1996. Used by permission of Tyndale House Publishers, Inc., Wheaton, Illinois 60189. All rights reserved.

Scripture quotations marked NASB are taken from the New American Standard Bible®. Copyright © 1960, 1963, 1968, 1971, 1972, 1973, 1975, 1977, 1995 by Lockman Foundation.™ Used by permission. (www.Lockman.org)

Page design by Mark L. Mabry

Library of Congress Control Number: 2011929836

ISBN: 9781595553638

Printed in the United States of America

11 12 13 14 15 RRD 6 5 4 3 2 1

For Brandy, who gave me a card at Fusion and has held my attention ever since. This journey is infinitely sweeter with you.

For Christy, who listened to my ramblings on the baseball field at Toccoa and has faithfully been there to watch much of it come true.

CONTENTS

CONTENTS

FOREWORD

The irony: two upstart Aussies from tiny towns half a world away wind up leading high impact churches in two of the most significant cities in North America. Only God!

Darren Whitehead and Jon Tyson are deep thinking Christ followers with a bias for action in the world. A rare combination these days. They are both leaders and communicators, visionaries and "get stuff done for God" guys. Extremely rare.

I have had the privilege of working closely with Darren at Willow Creek Community Church for over seven years. He is thoughtful, relationally intelligent, and one of the hardest working young leaders I know.

In *Rumors of God*, Darren and Jon have somehow succeeded in slipping 3–D glasses over our eyes. The results are that passages from Scripture come alive in ways that will impact readers for a long time.

I salute the efforts of these young mates and pray that readers will be as stretched in their minds and hearts as I have been.

Bill Hybels
Senior Pastor
Willow Creek Community Church
Chairman, Willow Creek Association

AUTHORS' NOTE

In life when something really good or really bad happens, we all have someone we call first. This year (2011) marks the twentieth year of us becoming mates. During the last two decades we have made literally hundreds of those "first" calls to each other. When you immigrate to the other side of the world, you forfeit personal history and tenured relationships. You basically start all over again. Our friendship is the only one that we both have in this country that predates our move. Even our wives have only known us since our move to the States. This unusual dynamic has forged something unique.

We met as teenagers at a youth camp in Mt. Barker, South Australia. Both of us came for the girls. In fact our first-ever collaboration was sneaking into the girls' sleeping quarters during the church service and piling up more than fifty mattresses into the center of the room. (Our second partnership was mopping all the bathrooms after we got caught!) Little did we know that we would one day be pastors in churches in two of America's largest cities.

A lot of life has happened in the last twenty years. We have been part of each other's weddings, have shown up when each other's kids were born, and have journeyed together through highs and lows. Through all the changes, we have had one tradition that dates back to our early days in Australia. When either of us senses that God is ending a ministry assignment, closing one door and opening another, we travel to that one's city and sit in the back of the empty church auditorium together. We spend several unhurried hours sitting in the quiet and telling stories of what God has done in that season. We try to drink deeply of the moment before a new chapter begins.

So now we're literally writing chapters together. Although we wrote in one voice, we occasionally delineate who is telling the story for the benefit of you, the reader.

We wrote this book because we love the church. Many have the sense that the greatest days of the church are in the past. We humbly disagree. This book is our small rebellion against that notion. We believe that if you listen to the rumors of God, you will hear that God is doing something new in the church. We long to confirm those rumors with our lives.

Here's to what's to come.

Cheers.

Darren Whitehead

Jon Tyson

CHAPTER 1

THE SCULPTOR'S SHOP

RUMORS OF ABUNDANT LIFE

> LORD, *I have heard of your fame;*
> *I stand in awe of your deeds,* LORD.
> *Renew them in our day,*
> *in our time make them known;*
> *in wrath remember mercy.*
>
> —the prayer of the prophet Habakkuk

The first couple of rows at church that morning held a unique assortment of women. They whispered nervously to each other before the service started, obviously feeling a little out of place and probably wondering if they should have come in the first place. Not your typical church attendees, these women would likely be going from the church to other, darker, environments;

but they had come on this day to celebrate the baptism of one of their compatriots, Rebecca. She, too, had a sordid past but today was a new beginning.

My (Darren) friend Catherine, on the other hand, had a past no one would be ashamed of. She grew up on a steady diet of Bible study and small-group experiences, going to church every week. She was actively involved in the children's ministry and found great community in the student ministries. By the time she reached her twenties, however, she felt disillusioned. After two decades of throwing herself into the Christian subculture and trying to grow spiritually, her faith seemed stagnant—she sensed there was something more to following Jesus.

In addition to this, the stories and accounts in the Bible read like science fiction to her in that she didn't see much evidence of their impact in her world. She knew she wasn't the only one who felt like this, but no one else seemed to care. Catherine was bored, uninspired, and disappointed with her faith experience. She was in a rut. So she started to search for something else.

Catherine trained to become a professional makeup artist and began working in the modeling and entertainment industry in Chicago. This lifestyle was hip, fast paced, and fascinating. She often worked with celebrities and influential icons in the fashion industry. Still, something was missing.

One day an older lady from church called and invited her to join a team headed to Costa Rica to serve women who were trying to break out of prostitution. They would train the Costa Rican women with alternative life and career skills so they would have new options for employment. The woman explained that Catherine could teach them how to apply makeup in an attractive and subtle manner. Before she knew it, Catherine heard herself agreeing to the trip.

During those three months in Costa Rica, Catherine encountered something she had never experienced. Loving, serving, and believing in these women was the most alive she had ever felt. It quickened her. She began to reengage her faith and opened her heart to a whole new way of experiencing God, and when it came time to go home, she knew she could not simply return to the spiritual rut she was living in before the trip. Something in her had awakened. How, she wondered, could she continue this work stateside?

When Catherine returned to Chicago, she did some research and began a most unusual way of serving women. At a strip club in the city, she worked backstage applying the women's makeup before they went out and performed.

As she selflessly loved these women, she started to build relationships with them. One day she decided to offer sermons on CDs from our church. No pressure, she would just bring a box of CDs and set it backstage for anyone to borrow and then return for others to use.

Several months went by, and one evening a stripper named Rebecca began to show an interest in the CD box. She borrowed a couple of CDs and liked them. A week later she asked if she could borrow the whole box. "Sure!" Catherine said. Rebecca listened to the entire box in a matter of days, and when she returned the box, Catherine asked if she wanted to attend church with her.

"Would I be allowed in?" asked Rebecca.

"Of course you would. We would love to have you."

When Rebecca came with Catherine to our church, I met with them in the lobby and we sat together at a table.

"So, you're a pastor?" Rebecca asked.

"Yeah, I am."

She looked me right in the eye and asked, "Do you know what I do?"

"Yeah, I do."

"Catherine is trying to tell me that God loves people like me. People who . . . um, do what I do."

Tears welled up in her eyes, spilled over her long eyelashes, and started running down her cheeks. It was hard to fight back the tears myself.

"Yes, Rebecca, God loves you deeply."

"How can this be?" she asked, and then started to tell me some of the horrible things people often say to her and shout at her while she works. "I don't understand how God can love me. I don't even love myself."

"Rebecca, Jesus came to take away our sin and shame and replace it with grace and mercy. That is the good news—that is God's message."

That day Rebecca accepted God's forgiveness and opened her life to his irrational love. A few weeks later I baptized her at our church. I will never forget the expression on her face. She glowed with joy and childlike delight.

The first few rows of the auditorium were filled with strippers and other people from the club. They were cheering and shouting to support Rebecca's moment. Several of them were weeping, some were laughing and crying. I couldn't help but wonder what they were thinking as they watched our church embrace and love this woman, a stripper. I remember thinking this had to be a taste of the kingdom of God.

Rebecca stopped stripping. Catherine ended up training her in the makeup profession, and together they continued to serve the other women. They even started to play Christian worship music backstage as the women were getting ready. In a place that was filled with depravity, exploitation, and pain, the rumors of the God of love started to circulate.

When I asked Catherine how she would describe this experience. She replied, "It was like coming to life!"

COMING TO LIFE

Don't we all want what Catherine experienced? Something deep in the human heart breaks at the thought of a life of mediocrity. Our hearts cry out for life—new life. In his classic work *Mere Christianity*, C. S. Lewis used a striking metaphor to describe the Christian's experience of coming to life. He said: "And that is precisely what Christianity is about. The world is a great sculptor's shop. We are the statues and there is a rumor going round the shop that some of us are some day going to come to life."[1]

How would you describe your experience of faith? Perhaps to you the life described in the Scriptures feels more like a series of rumors than real life. Maybe you're stuck in a rut, like Catherine. Jesus said, "I have come that they may have life, and that they may have it more abundantly."[2] Does that describe your experience? If not, you're not alone.

In fact, many churches today are filled with people who might describe their faith as being as cold as a statue—lifeless. Although Christianity is growing in places like South America, China, and India, this is not the case in the United States. In America, Christianity's growth and influence seem to be waning, as "nonreligious" has become the fastest-growing religious category.[3]

You can almost feel the change happening. It's as if the

Western church is on a "fade to black" trajectory. Society seems to be drifting further and further into secular humanism and we, as Christians, feel powerless to do anything about it. Ironically, the culture grows increasingly more "spiritual" while the church grows increasingly more practical. No wonder most Americans say they're not interested in Christianity.

Not only do we seem to be missing a connection with the greater culture, we can't seem to find common ground within our own ranks. Church leaders love to tangle about their own subcultural debates: liberal versus conservative, attractional versus incarnational, the city versus the suburbs, evangelism versus social justice, secularism, sexuality, consumerism, globalization, hell, heaven, and universalism—just to name a few. It seems as if Christians talk a lot about *what* we are doing or *how* we are doing it, but don't discuss *why* any of it even matters.

Sometimes it feels like that scene in *Titanic*, when the string quartet continues to play their instruments as the ship sinks. They make every effort to avoid sliding off their chairs, while pretending not to notice the ship is going down.

It seems like the future of the Western church is hanging in the balance.

A RISING HOPE

The prophet Habakkuk lived in a time when the future of God's people was also hanging in the balance. There was prevalent sin and judgment within God's people, a growing ungodly world power and uncertainty with God's rule. The prophet captured the *why* of his generation when he prayed:

LORD, *I have heard of your fame;*
I stand in awe of your deeds, LORD.
Renew them in our day,
in our time make them known;
in wrath remember mercy.[4]

Habakkuk passionately verbalized the anguish of his time. He had heard rumors of God's fame, caught rumblings of God's deeds, but would not stop until he experienced the *reality* of the transcendent power of God in his life. Habakkuk started to cry out for something he had never seen. The cry of his heart was to see an awakening of the fame and deeds of God—in his day, in his time, in his generation.

When we were teenagers we experienced an awakening. We both grew up in a Christian tradition that was more defined by what you didn't do than by what you did. Christians prided themselves on abstaining from drinking, smoking, swearing, and dancing. This defined the Christian subculture.

Growing up in South Australia, Jon and I met in our late teens when we both started attending the same church youth group. Jon had recently become a Christian and I was discovering that God was not a series of religious rules and positive lifestyle principles. In fact, we were both captivated by an idea that was brand-new to us. God's strategy for redemption on the earth was to be carried out by the church.

The very same sleepy, uninspiring institution that we painstakingly endured growing up was actually the community that was anointed and called by God. It was astounding that right under our noses were the most compelling vision, mission, and cause that we had ever heard. Captured by this new reality, Jon and I started to pray together. We would often get up early and pray in our church parking lot, in the city, or on a hill overlooking the city, asking God to allow us to see the church become all that he had called her to be.

Independently, within six months of each other, Jon and I both moved to the United States to study and work. During the last thirteen years, Jon and I have been on staff at seven different churches. Today Jon is the senior pastor of Trinity Grace Church in New York City—a thriving, growing church with five neighborhood churches in the city. I am a teaching pastor at Willow Creek Community Church, one of the largest megachurches in North America. We moved to the United States because we believed the church in the Western world would be worked out in America.

Some would say we have ended up in diametrically opposed environments—a church planter in an urban context and a megachurch teaching pastor in the suburbs. What do these guys have in common? Our response: Twenty years of friendship, a mutual love for the church, and a desire to see the church reach her God-given potential. We are convinced we are living in a pivotal time in history. We want to see God do something truly historic in our day, in our time, in our generation.

We wrote this book because the thought of our generation going to the grave without seeing the fame and deeds of God filling the pages of our own stories and the story of the world is untenable. We believe God is writing an epic, global, redemptive story that every single one of us has been invited into.

We want to share our own experiences in life and ministry where we see people breaking free of spiritual ruts and coming to life, just like Catherine. We hope that as you read you will gain a clearer understanding of the cultural and spiritual obstacles the Western church faces and, more important, how we can overcome them. Every day in our ministries we see vivid signs of God's kingdom coming to earth. We pray God will ignite your hearts with the desire to see it in your life, in your church, and in your community.

May we echo the prayer of Habakkuk and see the church rise up in our day and in our time. We are convinced that God has something fresh that he wants to do, and we know that God rewards those who earnestly seek him. We want to experience the kind of faith we've only read about and heard about.

These are the stories of statues coming to life. The rumors are true.

CHAPTER 2

HOSTAGES OF THE MIND

Rumors of Another Dream

*[We] are being persuaded to spend money we don't have, on
things we don't need, to create impressions that won't last, on
people we don't care about.*

—Tim Jackson

*Now to him who is able to do immeasurably more than all
we ask or imagine, according to his power that is at work
within us.*

—St. Paul to the church in Ephesus

Daddy, Daddy!"

I (Darren) woke up to the wails of my three-year-old daughter. I winced at the clock by my bed: 3:02 a.m. Groggily I flopped out of bed and stumbled into my daughter's room.

"What's wrong, sweetie?" I muttered.

She motioned for me to pick her up, so I scooped her into my arms.

"What's wrong?"

She refused to answer and just buried her little face in my neck and sobbed. Her small body convulsed as she took deep breaths between wails.

"Did you have a bad dream?" I asked. She stopped crying for a second, looked up at me, and nodded with affirmation. Then she nestled her face back into my neck and started crying again.

"Sweetie, what did you dream about?"

She looked up again, "Minnie was mean to me!"

"Minnie?" I asked. "Who's Minnie?"

"You know, Daddy . . . Minnie Mouse!"

I whispered a few comforting phrases that dads say to their little girls and eventually laid her back in her bed, fast asleep once more.

As I was walking back to my room, I was struck by the thought, *My daughter was dreaming about Minnie Mouse! An animated cartoon character!* Someone else created Minnie Mouse, yet when my daughter closes her eyes and sleeps, Minnie shows up in her dreams. She doesn't dream with her own characters, she dreams with someone else's. As I was climbing back into bed it hit me: my daughter's imagination had been taken captive.

I HAVE A DREAM

What about you? What do you want? What do you dream about? When your mind is left to wander, what does it involuntarily drift toward? What scenarios do you find yourself imagining? If God were a cosmic genie and you could ask him for anything, what would you ask for?

Let me guess. You would like to have more money—financial stability. A comfortable living environment would be nice, perhaps a newer car. You'd have a progressing career, be respected in your field. You'd like to have emotionally healthy friends, who are energetic, encouraging, spontaneous, and fun. Maybe you'd wish to change something about your appearance—lose a few pounds, be taller, more athletic. If you're single, you might desire to find a life partner, someone supportive, kind, and attractive (not just on the inside).

Maybe you want to have kids. Or maybe you already have kids, and you want them to be well-educated, high-functioning, successful, well-mannered children who do better in school than your friends' kids.

Or perhaps you'd like to be famous and influence millions of people around the world for the greater good.

There's nothing inherently wrong with these dreams. They are the carrots the media dangle in front of us. But what's interesting is that, for the most part, the desires and dreams of Christians are the same as non-Christians'. Essentially we are dreaming and longing for the same things. This seems odd—shouldn't we be different from non-Christians? Shouldn't our dreams be fueled by a different story?

Maybe we're in worse shape than we thought—maybe we don't even know what to wish for. Maybe *our* imaginations have been taken captive by the world.

Just as my daughter's imagination is full of Disney characters, our imaginations are full of the characters of the world. The powerful cultural forces of the media and entertainment seize our dreams and hopes for the future. We find ourselves believing the definitions of success, happiness, and fulfillment given to us by the world.

In his book *Culture Jam: The Uncooling of America*, Kalle Lasn says:

> American culture is no longer created by the people. A free authentic life is no longer possible in America today. We are being manipulated in the most insidious ways. Our emotions, core values and personalities are under siege from media and cultural forces too complex to decode. A continuous product message has woven itself into the very fabric of our existence. Most North Americans now live designer lives. Sleep, eat, sit in a car, work, shop, eat, watch TV, sleep again. I doubt that there's more than a handful of free, spontaneous minutes anywhere in that cycle. We ourselves have been branded.

Lasn points out that life in America is like life in a cult. We act and behave in ways we did not consciously choose:

> "Dreams" by definition are supposed to be unique and imaginative. Yet the bulk of our population is dreaming the same dream. It's a dream of wealth, power, fame, plenty of sex and exciting recreational opportunities.[1]

When the entire culture is dreaming the same thing, imagination has been taken captive. An alternative dream requires animation by a different narrative.

Many of us have been sold this dream since we were children, discipled by a series of values, ideals, desires, and worldviews. Our lifestyle choices belie our conscious and subconscious assumptions. Perhaps no organization over the last couple of generations has formed our worldview more than the creator of Minnie Mouse, the Walt Disney company.

Disney Corporation owns the television networks ABC, ESPN, the Discovery Channel, A&E, and, of course, the Disney Channel. With winsome characters like Mickey Mouse and Winnie the Pooh all the way to the Jonas Brothers, Hannah Montana, and *High School Musical*, Walt Disney is raising America's children.

When we were growing up, we watched a TV show on Sunday nights called *The Wonderful World of Disney*. The musical theme of that show was from *Pinocchio*: "When you wish upon a star, your dreams come true." Walt Disney wanted to create a faux reality, a utopian world free of pain and complexity.

"In numerous ways," wrote professor and author Neil Gabler, "Disney struck what may be the very fundament of entertainment: the promise of a perfect world that conforms to our wishes."[2]

In Walt Disney's early years, he was deep in debt and had a miserable marriage with an unsupportive wife. So he wanted to create a world of escape. Walt Disney often took other cultural stories or fables and adapted them to reflect his desires of utopian escapism from the miserable realities of his life.

The story of Pinocchio, for example, was originally an Italian fable designed to warn children against dishonesty. In the original story, Pinocchio murders his conscience, "Jiminy Cricket," by stomping him under his foot. The story ends when Pinocchio dies a gruesome death—he is hung, killed as a result of his narcissism. Walt Disney took this and countless other stories—many originally told to help form a child's character—and changed them all to essentially the same story: the protagonist's deepest desires come true and he or she lives happily ever after. Walt Disney made us believe we could have anything we want.

Is it any wonder that young people grow up with a sense of entitlement? They have each been told they are the most important person in the world and *deserve* to have everything they've ever wanted. They are sold the idea that if they get everything they want, they will be happy. Now that Disney has raised several generations, we can see that this is simply not true.

Like Disney, McDonald's marketers are also experts in captivating young minds. Researchers at the Stanford University School of Medicine and Lucile Packard Children's Hospital conducted a study with children aged three to five. They presented the kids with two sets of chicken nuggets, one wrapped in McDonald's packaging and the other in plain packaging. After the children ate, the researchers asked them, "Which group of nuggets tasted better?" The nuggets were *exactly* the same, only the packaging was different.

The study found the overwhelming majority of children preferred the taste of the nuggets in the McDonald's packaging over the unbranded nuggets, despite the fact that the food was no different. The director of the Center for Healthy Weight at Lucile Packard Children's Hospital, Thomas Robinson, reported: "Kids don't just ask for the food from McDonald's, they actually believe that the chicken nugget they think is from McDonald's tastes better than an identical, unbranded nugget."[3]

This test was repeated with food items not usually associated with the McDonald's menu. When food items like carrots, milk, and apple juice were presented, the taste buds of three-year-olds were already imagining a superior taste.[4]

Many global brands and large corporations now recruit expert child psychologists to work exclusively for their companies, paying them not to *determine* the preferences of children, but to *manipulate* the emotional triggers in children. Lucy Hughes, vice president of Initiative Media, said companies can manipulate consumers into buying their products if they can get children to nag their parents. According to a leading expert on branding, 80 percent of all global brands now deploy a "tween strategy."[5]

A task force of the American Psychological Association (APA) recommended restrictions on advertising that targets children under the age of eight, based on research showing that children under this age are unable to critically comprehend televised advertising messages and are prone to accept advertiser messages as truthful, accurate, and unbiased.[6] The average North American views more than three thousand ads per day.[7] Not just on billboards or television or the Web, but now ads on gas pumps and washroom stalls and checkouts in grocery stores clutter our minds with targeted messages telling us what we want.

More than ever, other people and organizations make our choices for us. With our imaginations captive, we are quite literally programmed to want certain things. We think we need these items because the advertising world tells us we do. And so we live and work in order to try to bring ourselves to life. All the while our hearts and souls atrophy.

ROTTEN APPLES

Why do we pine for the things of this world as we do? Perhaps it's because we have yet to find all we need in Christ himself. Jesus used the example of a child helplessly asking a parent for a food. "Which of you, if your son asks for bread, will give him a stone? Or if he asks for a fish, will give him a snake? If you, then, though you are evil, know how to give good gifts to your children, how much more will your Father in heaven give good gifts to those who ask him?"[8]

Every parent in their right mind wants to love and provide for their children. It's the same with God. As our heavenly Father he wants to give us good gifts, but we don't ask. Our attention has drifted from God—and rested on the trappings of the world. With our imaginations held captive, we think all we need is sex, money, and power. All the while, our Father has something better and is waiting for us to simply ask.

Not long ago I (Darren) took two of my daughters apple picking. At ages three and one, they had never seen apples growing on trees before, let alone handpicked them. It was a perfect autumn day, not a cloud in the sky, and the trees were bursting with ripe, delicious fruit. As we walked toward the rows of trees, one of my daughters started running ahead of us. She bent down, and finding a rotten apple on the ground started eating it. As I got closer, I discovered it was an apple that someone had taken a bite from and dropped on the ground a few days earlier.

"Don't eat that!" I shouted. She gave me a dumbfounded look. I grabbed the apple and threw it away.

Through her tears she whimpered, "That was my apple, Daddy."

"We don't eat apples from the ground . . . and there's no need to tell Mommy about this! Look at these trees," I said as she lifted her eyes to the thousands of apples surrounding her on the branches. I grabbed her hand and led her over to a tree with apples right at her height. "Here, try one of these."

She reached out her little hands and grabbed a ripe Red Delicious that was bursting with color. She snapped it off the tree, and I showed her how to shine it on her shirt. Then, with a smile of anticipation, she opened her mouth and sank her teeth into the red fruit. With a mouth full of apple, juice dripping from her chin, she chimed, "It's good!"

I said, "Yeah, it's good. Dad knows best, right?"

She smiled and nodded.

All too often we turn down the infinitely valuable in exchange for the trivial. C. S. Lewis put it like this: "We are . . . like an ignorant child who wants to go on making mud pies in a slum because he cannot imagine what is meant by the offer of a holiday at the sea. We are far too easily pleased."[9]

Why aren't more of us asking, seeking, and knocking? Or the better question may be, why aren't more of us receiving, finding, and opening? James, the half brother of Jesus, answered that question in two ways. First he said, "You do not have, because you do not ask God."[10]

Life is busy. We live like slaves to our fast-paced, suffocating schedules. There's so much more that God wants to give, tell, and show us, but we simply don't ask. We spend our energy and time in triviality, splashing in the shallow end of our souls.

In the very next verse, James pointed to a second reason: "When you ask, you do not receive, because you ask with wrong motives, that you may spend what you get on your pleasures."[11] James powerfully exposes the tendency of the human heart to try to coerce and manipulate God to upgrade the comfort of our lives.

INTERRUPTION OR INTERVENTION

If we're not careful, the current of the world will carry us along. Without knowing it, we will close off our lives to the radical movement of God's Spirit and kingdom. If you keep living like you are right now, what will be the outcome of your life? Apart from a financial, relational, or health crisis, you have probably established your values, patterns, and behaviors—your own personal brand of life. So apart from some major unforeseen crisis, you'll continue on the same path.

You might tweak your life a little, you might upgrade a bit; but, for the most part, you're going to keep living as you're living right now for the rest of your life. We map out the way we want things to go and manage our lives to make sure they get there. Instead of being open to the promptings of the Spirit, God stepping into our lives seems more like an *interruption* than an *intervention*. We really only want God to step in if he gives us what we want. But Jesus calls us to a better way. Another dream. Beyond what is simply plausible to what is possible. Breaking free from our past or even our present to a whole new way of life—an unimagined future.

Kelly moved to New York City from a sleepy small town in Oklahoma. She came as a student, graduated from a respected design school, and secured a job with a major clothing brand in the fashion industry. Her dream was to keep progressing in her career and as her income increased so would her standard of living. Sometimes she would walk through the prestigious neighborhoods of the Upper East Side and imagine how it would feel to pull out her keys and enter her four-story brownstone. She watched people come and go from their multimillion-dollar homes and tried to guess what they did for a living and how they became so successful.

One Sunday evening a regular attendee of our (Jon's) church brought Kelly to our Upper West Side neighborhood church service. Kelly had grown up attending a little church in Oklahoma but had not been in more than ten years. She was amazed that people in our community were so passionate about helping under-resourced families in some of the most dangerous neighborhoods in New York. She had never seen anything like it—young, gifted, and driven professionals wanting to steward their privilege on behalf of the poor.

Kelly was drawn to this intriguing faith community. Over the next year Kelly never missed a Sunday night at church. She renewed her faith commitment to Jesus and started to take time regularly to ask God what he wanted for her life. She would some-times say that she could feel the goals, desires, and hopes in her life start to fade and be replaced by infinitely greater dreams.

After eighteen months in our church, Kelly moved to a neighborhood in the South Bronx, widely recognized as one of the most dangerous neighborhoods in the country. Kelly moved into an apartment building and started to befriend people in the community. The kids in this neighborhood had seen only one way of life—a life centered on gangs, drugs, violence, prostitution, and crime. Kelly knew that if someone didn't intervene, the future of these children would be defined by these realities. So Kelly had an idea. She started spending time with the neighborhood kids and asking them: "If you could do anything with your life what would it be?"

Most of the kids had never imagined a future of possibilities. So they often took a few weeks to think about it. But soon kids were saying they wanted to be musicians and doctors and fire-fighters and Wall Street bankers. Every time a child mentioned a new profession to Kelly, she contacted someone in our church who was already working in that particular industry and asked them to meet with these kids.

An eleven-year-old boy whose dream was to be a musician now receives free bass lessons from one of the most respected bass players in Manhattan. And a twelve-year-old girl, who wants to be a graphic artist, meets weekly with a graphic designer who works for a national fashion magazine.

Kelly's vision was to liberate the imaginations of these children, to let them dream new dreams, and hope for a better future.

This is what God wants to do for us. Most of us are trapped in a cultural ghetto. The only things we can imagine are luxury, affluence, prestige, and success. Jesus entered the world to expand our horizon of possibility, to recover the forgotten passions of our heart, and to help leverage our gifts for his dream of restoration and hope. He wants to unleash our imaginations.

UNLEASH YOUR IMAGINATION

In the Lord's Prayer, Jesus highlighted the importance of getting things in order. When Jesus taught his followers how to pray he said, "May your kingdom come, your will be done on earth as it is in heaven. Then, give us this day our daily bread."[12] Most of us want to reverse this order. Our instinctive prayer is "give us our daily bread and hopefully that will be your will on earth." Jesus communicated the idea here to ask God to transform our desires and our hearts. "May it be as heaven wants."

When our hearts align with what heaven wants, then we're ready to ask, and *then* God will supply our needs. The prayer says: "Teach us what to ask for." When we learn what to ask God for, then our minds and hearts will not be focused on the things the world offers, but on the things above.[13] It's the things above that set our imaginations free.

When I attended Sunday school as a kid, we memorized 1 Corinthians 2:9: "No eye has seen, no ear has heard, no mind has conceived what God has prepared for those who love him" (NIV 1984). But the very next verse was almost never mentioned:"But God has revealed it to us by his Spirit." Our dream is not limited to what our culture puts forth. We dream from a place our culture cannot access. God wants to *reveal* these dreams to us. He wants to release our minds; he wants us to imagine a whole other way to live.

The movement of Jesus is supposed to be defined by dreamers and visionaries. As Peter said on the day the church began in Jerusalem: "In the last days, God says, I will pour my Spirit out on all people. Your sons and daughters will prophesy, your young men will see visions, your old men will dream dreams."[14]

To those who will listen, God wants to reveal creative new ways to live. This breathes new possibility into the church. Cynical and jaded young people will receive a vision for their future. Disappointed and disillusioned older people will recover their dreams. Don't you want that—the kingdom of God coming to rupture our present reality? With the Spirit in our midst the church should literally be the most creative place on earth.

Jesus said, "May your will be done on earth as it is in heaven." It's the call for us to bring the kingdom of God to our lives and communities. It's pulling the future into the present. Why wouldn't God do this? These dreamers and visionaries who seek after God often become those who shape human history.

You are invited to ask for the kingdom to come.

RUMORS OF ANOTHER DREAM

When I (Darren) graduated from school, I started working in the sales office of a steel manufacturing company. There were several hundred people on this sales floor. I was the only Christian in the office, and everyone knew it. I was happily attending my church when one day a pastor challenged me to start seeking God. During this time I lived with a couple of twenty-something guys, so I was often distracted in my prayer life. I started to set my alarm for 3:00 a.m. to get out of bed and spend time in prayer in the silence of the early morning. Then I went back to sleep.

One morning as I was praying, I started to imagine people in my office having experiences of spiritual awakening. Not long after that during a workday I felt a strong prompting to pray. So, as weird as this may sound, I got up from my desk and walked downstairs to the bathroom. I stepped into the first stall, closed the door, got on my knees, and prayed, "God, may your kingdom come in this office. May you do more than I could possibly think or imagine. May you show up in this place. I want to believe for what is actually possible." I vividly remember praying that prayer.

During the next few weeks, one of my coworkers, Matt, started to show interest in faith and spiritual conversations; so I invited him to come to church with me. He had never stepped foot in a church in his life. During the service I continuously prayed that he would be aware of God's presence.

After the service we went out for dinner. As we ate together he bombarded me with questions about the Bible, about God, and about my faith journey. We discussed theological concepts like grace, sin, repentance, forgiveness, atonement, and the sacrifice of Jesus. As we were walking back to the car, we passed by a bus stop, and I remember sensing a prompting from God to ask Matt if he wanted to invite God into his life.

"It seems that God is speaking to you," I said. "Do you want to pray and invite him to lead your life?"

He said, "Yeah, I really do!" So Matt and I knelt together on the sidewalk, next to the bus stop, and he opened his heart to the grace of God and asked Jesus to lead his life.

I remember going to work the next day with a profound awareness of God's presence and God's desire to make himself known. I thought: God rewards those who earnestly seek him.[15]

How do we see more of the reality and presence of God in our lives? We must prioritize seeking God—we will not accidently drift into it. We must intentionally, deliberately, earnestly make seeking God a priority in the way we spend our time.

When we ask, seek, and knock, God will transform our desires, awaken our hearts, and set our imaginations free.

Recently, as I was tucking my daughter into bed, she asked, "Daddy, will you pray that I have good dreams tonight?"

So I held her tiny hands and I prayed that God would fill my daughter's little mind with visions of his kingdom. I asked God to unleash her imagination, and I prayed that her dreams would be fueled by the unlimited possibilities of heaven.

And this is our prayer for you: May the dreams and visions of the church not just be fueled by Western culture, but may they be animated by an undeniable taste of the kingdom of God.

May God teach us what to ask for, and may we be a people who are not only known for asking, seeking, and knocking, but also known for receiving, finding, and opening.

And most of all may you discover that these rumors of God are true as you pursue his fame and deeds in our time.

In Jesus' name. Amen.

CHAPTER 3

THE GREAT REVERSAL

Rumors of Generosity

Keep your lives free from the love of money and be content with what you have, because God has said, "Never will I leave you; never will I forsake you."

—the author of Hebrews

Money flows effortlessly to that which is its God.

—Timothy Keller

Somebody said to me, "But the Beatles were anti-materialistic." That's a huge myth. John and I literally used to sit down and say, "Now, let's write a swimming pool."

—Paul McCartney

We have a friend who is a professional athlete. He has represented the United States at three different Olympic games. He currently holds the U. S. record for the fastest 50k. At a recent dinner we asked him about the level of discipline required to keep his body conditioned to compete at this level.

He explained that it takes an extraordinary amount of commitment. Olympic athletes turn down social opportunities in order to go to bed early, get out of bed before the sun comes up, limit their diets to include the perfect blend of protein, fiber, complex carbohydrates, and nutrients. And why do they do this? The medal. The medal is the dream. The fantasy of winning an Olympic medal is what propels these athletes forward. But as we know, all medals are not created equal. *USA Today* cited a report that surveyed the happiness and contentment level of the gold, silver, and bronze medal winners. No surprises, the happiest athletes were the gold medalists. The next result, however, may surprise you. You may think the silver medalists were next on the happiness scale. They weren't. The bronze medalists were happier than the silver medalists.[1]

The silver medalists think, *I came so close to winning gold*. The bronze medalists think, *I almost didn't get a medal—I'm grateful to be on the podium*. One reflects on what they have, the other reflects on what they don't have. The third-place athlete is happier than the second-place athlete. Psychologists describe this as counterfactual thinking. It's the "I could have" or "I should have" state of mind.

As Western Christians we sometimes suffer from this "silver medal syndrome." Though we have the highest standard of living in recorded history, we never quite seem to have enough.

Enough?

In his book *Enough: True Measures of Money, Business, and Life*, John C. Bogle recounts an event that highlights the importance of contentment.

At a party given by a billionaire on Shelter Island, Kurt Vonnegut informs his pal, Joseph Heller, that their host, a hedge fund manager, had made more money in a single day than Heller had earned from his wildly popular novel *Catch-22* over its whole history. Heller responds. "Yes, but I have something he will never have . . . enough."[2]

If we always compare ourselves with those in financial brackets above us, we will never feel content. We look above us and think that we don't have enough. And our culture works hard to keep us looking up. But when we take a moment to realize the financial brackets of those below us, we gain immediate perspective. The United States has just 5 percent of the world's population but consumes 30 percent of the world's resources. If the whole world consumed at the rate of the United States, we would need three, four, or five planets just to accommodate everything.

If you own a car, no matter what kind, you're among only 8 percent of the world. The rest of the world—92 percent—would be envious of your fortune.

It has been estimated that 1.1 billion people don't have access to clean drinking water.[3] They would probably look at us and say, "We can't imagine not having to walk six miles for water, but simply turning on a tap in our homes." Severe hunger afflicts 862 million people each year. Some experts say to completely solve global hunger would cost about thirty billion dollars a year. Americans spend more than that each year on pizza. For much of the world, *we* are the ones living the dream.

RUNNING WITH THE WORLD

In the Sermon on the Mount, Jesus told his followers: "Do not worry about your life, what you will eat or drink; or about your body; what you will wear. Is not life more important than food, and the body more than clothes?. . . So do not worry saying 'What shall we eat?' or 'What shall we drink?' or 'What shall we wear?' For the pagans run after these things, and your heavenly Father knows that you need them. But seek first his kingdom and his righteousness, and all these things will be given to you as well."[4]

The great temptation of our culture is to run after the same things that everyone else does. Rather than trusting God to supply our needs, we get caught in the frenzy of accumulation. Like a person in a crowd at a "black Friday" sale, God gets pushed to the side. In contrast to this mind-set, Jesus says life is more important than material pursuits.

The apostle Paul challenged Timothy with these words: "Command those who are rich in this present world not to be arrogant nor to put their hope in wealth, which is so uncertain, but to put their hope in God, who richly provides us with everything for our enjoyment."[5] He then instructed Timothy to command the rich to "do good, to be rich in good deeds, and to be generous and willing to share. In this way they will lay up treasure for themselves as a firm foundation for the coming age, so that they may take hold of the life that is truly life."[6]

The phrase "take hold of the life that is truly life" is profound. Paul indicates that there is a unique correlation between what we do with our money and the quality of life we experience. We are pushed to believe that life in all its fullness is to be found in an abundance of possessions. But Paul says the opposite. The *life that is truly life* is found in how we steward our resources, not in hoarding them.

WHERE YOUR TREASURE IS

I (Jon) once heard Tim Keller say, "Money flows effortlessly to that which is its God." So I devised a short test to see where we would like our money to flow.

Imagine I were to say to you, "I want you to set aside 10 percent of your income each month, for the purpose of taking a luxury trip to Paris." What is your emotional response?

Or imagine, "I want you to set aside 10 percent of your income each month to upgrade all the technology in your life to the latest versions." Your emotional response now?

Or again, "I want you to set aside 10 percent of your income each month to update your wardrobe. You can spend all you have saved on two giant sales each year." What is your emotional response?

Now tell me your emotional response to the following:

"I want you to set aside 10 percent of your income each month to help the unemployed in your church."

"I want you to set aside 10 percent of your income each month to give to the homeless shelter."

"I want you to set aside 10 percent of your income each month to help pay off the debts of the people in your small group."

If we were to be honest, for a lot of us, it would be safe to say that we are doing quite well in our race with the world. Most of our attention and affection and energy are flowing toward the same things as the world's. Indeed, money flows effortlessly to that which is its God.

CULTIVATING DISCONTENTMENT

How did this happen to us? How did we get to the point where radical generosity is only a rumor in the church and not our current reality? Why are our financial habits so similar to the world's habits? Victor Lebow, an economist from the last century, observed how the seeds of consumer culture were being sown in his day, and how they would ultimately bear fruit in all of our lives. He famously said, "Our enormously productive economy . . . demands that we make consumption our way of life, that we convert the buying and use of goods into rituals, that we seek our spiritual satisfaction, our ego satisfaction, in consumption . . . we need things consumed, burned up, replaced, and discarded at an ever-accelerating rate."[7]

This pressure to spiritualize our purchases often results in God's life being choked out of our souls.

In her insightful book *The Story of Stuff*, Annie Leonard pulls back the curtain to further expose how hyperconsumption has come to control our lives. After World War II, marketers, manufacturers, and economists got together and talked openly about how they could get Americans to become obsessive consumers.[8] The outcome was a two-pronged strategy that had a dramatic effect on American life.

1. Planned Obsolescence

Planned obsolescence is worked into the manufacturing of the goods that we buy. Products are designed to wear out quickly and then be thrown away. This is a delicate business. Manufacturers had to walk a fine line. If things wore out too quickly, consumers would feel taken advantage of, but if they didn't wear out quickly enough, then not enough product would be moved. So with careful research and experimentation, manufacturers conspired to design poor-quality products that, after a short period, we are conditioned to happily replace. Although we occasionally say things like "they don't make 'em like they used to," we have come to expect that this is simply the way things are.

It has been sixty years since this subversive plan was initiated, and today's manufacturers have it down to an art. Even our mobile phones, computers, and appliances only last a couple of years. We live in the disposable age. But what do you do with the rare consumers who take exceptional care of the things they own?

2. Perceived Obsolescence

This is the idea of fashion and trends. Trends, in many ways, dictate our cultural ebb and flow. Based on a fear of being left out and left behind, we feel immense pressure to keep up with the fashionable moment. Styles are continually changing, technology is continually evolving, and the "missing out" motivates us to purchase, regardless of the current state of our goods. And so the cycle continues. In an effort to resist this, my father refused to buy new suits. For six or seven years, he did the ugly stroll, but every ninth or tenth year, he rode out the fashion reincarnation and was a style icon!

A NEW CULTURAL RHYTHM

After describing the plan to make products obsolete, Leonard goes on to say that most of us are now caught up in a new cultural rhythm. Instead of living like previous generations—resting, enjoying our families, joining social groups, and contributing to the greater good of society—our lives are now reduced to this simple rhythm: Work. Watch. Spend. Repeat.

Work: We work hard all week only to come home exhausted. With little emotional margin left, we seek things to numb and relax us. We often default to the television.

Watch: Sitting in front of the TV, our media programming is filled with carefully selected product placement. During the course of ten hours, American viewers will see approximately three hours of advertising, twice what they would have seen in the 1960s.

Spend: When we do get time off, our favorite place to relax and connect is at the mall. The products we have seen are then available for immediate purchase. We often overextend ourselves financially to get these products. By doing so, we incur debt that causes us to work longer, more demanding hours.

Repeat. Repeat. Repeat.

How do we break free from this cycle? How do we resist the pressure of the age? How do we take hold of the life that is truly life—the life that is rumored in the Scriptures? Jesus proposed some radical solutions.

A Secret Economy

Giving is the first thing to do in breaking the cycle of greed and taking hold of real life. This may seem intuitive, but it's not so simple. Even giving has been taken captive by the culture of consumption. Think about how economic language has entered into our relationships. We talk about "relational bank accounts"—owing people favors, paying others back, and making emotional deposits. In fact it seems almost impossible to relate to others without pulling out a spreadsheet and calculating the cost-to-benefit ratio of the friendship. French philosopher Jacques Derrida articulated the economic impact of relationships in his teaching about "the gift."

He claimed that all giving creates unintentional economic repercussions. Whenever somebody offers a gift, it is almost impossible to receive it freely. We unintentionally feel that we are in that person's debt. Consider a simple dinner invitation. If someone has you over for dinner, every time you see that person, you probably feel obligated to invite him or her over. This is how Derrida explained it:

> As soon as a gift is identified as a gift, with the meaning of a gift, then it is canceled as a gift. It is reintroduced into the cycle of an exchange and destroyed as a gift. As soon as the donee knows it is a gift, he already thanks the donor, and cancels the gift. As soon as the donor is conscious of giving, he himself thanks himself and again cancels the gift by reinscribing it into a circle, an economic circle.[9]

Derrida seems to break down giving into an equation.

Giver + Gift + Recipient=Obligated gift in return

We see this at work everywhere in our world. From nonprofit organizations named after celebrities to hospital wings named after generous donors, people seem to expect some kind of return for their generosity. This even shows up in the church. Large financial donors have access to pastors and staff, while the general attendee is screened out through assistants and schedules. Enter the brilliance of Jesus' words in the Sermon on the Mount:

> Be careful not to practice your acts of righteousness in front of others to be seen by them. If you do, you will have no reward from your Father in heaven. So when you give to the needy, do not announce it with trumpets, as the hypocrites do in the synagogues and on the streets, to be honored by others. Truly I tell you, they have received their reward in full. But when you give to the needy, do not let your left hand know what your right hand is doing.[10]

Jesus' insight tells us that if we want to change the commodified friendships that our world is built on, we have to change the relational formula.

Secret Giver + Gift + Recipient=Freedom of the heart

When we give in secret, we break the cycle of obligation that is so often present in our relationships. Have you ever had someone anonymously give you money? It's an interesting experience. Everything within us longs to know who gave it, so that we can thank them and honor them and try to pay them back. Left without someone to thank, all we can do is look to God and rejoice—and humbly learn to receive.

Have you ever given in secret? It does such a powerful work. Although there is a tendency to want to identify ourselves as the source, giving in secret liberates us from the praises of people and gives us joy in watching others receive. This sort of giving has the power to transform our hearts and break us out of the rut that we often find ourselves in.

When I (Jon) was a college student in Texas, I worked part-time as a youth pastor and could only afford to live in a trailer park. I was sometimes called upon to preach and share in the larger church, but I couldn't afford nice clothes. One of the other pastors wore designer brands and decided to help me. He gave me a bag of his older shirts and I received them with joy. I wore one of his shirts to a Sunday service, where he proceeded to point out that he had given it to me to help me out. Everyone looked at me and I was humiliated. Every time I wore one of his shirts he pointed out how good I looked in his old clothes. I stopped wearing them.

Then one day a box from an anonymous sender arrived at my house. It was filled with new, brand name shirts, in my size. I wore those shirts every day with my head held high, simply thankful to God that he had met my needs. I didn't feel as if I owed anyone anything, and that simple act of generosity sincerely touched my heart.

Eternal Portfolios

The second thing Jesus does to liberate our hearts is to expand our portfolios from the temporary to the eternal. Because of the Resurrection and Jesus defeating the grave, we now have the gift of living with him forever. Rather than this being a peripheral doctrine, it can become a powerful force for releasing generosity.

People who only consider this life for their money have a tendency toward a scarcity mentality: "My limited resources must be spent in my lifetime or I'm not getting the best out of life." The Scriptures tell us the opposite. God has unlimited riches in Christ Jesus, and we have an eternal inheritance kept for us in heaven. This enables us to be incredibly generous with what we have in our short lives here. This epiphany played out in the book of Acts, when the believers first realized the Resurrection's tremendous implications for their lives.

> All the believers were one in heart and mind. No one claimed that any of their possessions was their own, but they shared everything they had. With great power the apostles continued to testify to the resurrection of the Lord Jesus. And God's grace was so powerfully at work in them all that there were no needy persons among them. For from time to time those who owned land or houses sold them, brought the money from the sales and put it at the apostles' feet, and it was distributed to anyone who had need.[11]

Jesus' resurrection changes everything. One of the first places it manifests itself is in radical generosity.

Early on in my (Jon's) ministry as a youth pastor, we had the privilege of reaching some of the most on-the-fringe kids I had ever met. Our youth group had a reputation as the "Gothic" youth group, and word on the street was, "Don't send your kids there, it is total chaos." Was it total chaos? Yes. But it was also the most pure and beautiful thing I had been a part of. The highlight of my week was taking these "Emo" and "Goth" kids out for pizza after the youth service. I picked up and dropped off these students from their homes in an old beat-up minivan. One day the inevitable happened. The old minivan died. The thing that concerned me the most was not the lack of resources I had for a new car, but the fact that this vital ministry would not continue. So I prayed. I asked God for a new car.

About a week later, my wife and I were having dinner with some friends from the church. They are an amazing couple, and we had a great time. At the end of the night, we were getting ready to leave, and they walked us out to the driveway. We walked past their car—a top-of-the-line, fully loaded minivan. The husband suddenly stopped and said, "I need to tell you a story. Last week I was on a business trip to Seattle. I was flying back, somewhere over the Midwest, when God spoke to me clearly and told me to give you our van."

His wife chimed in: "Around the same time, I was finishing up hosting a dinner party, when I felt God prompt me to give you our new van. The first thing I did when my husband got home was tell him, 'I think we are supposed to give the Tysons our new van.' He said he felt the same thing!"

So standing there, they handed us the keys to a fully loaded, leather trimmed minivan (with twin DVD players!) and said, "This is yours. It's a gift from God. We will sort the paperwork out later."

We were dumbfounded. In shock, we took the keys and drove home. We laughed and cried. Not just that God had heard our prayers, but that we could continue to serve these kids. The next week when we picked up the kids, they were stunned. That car became a community gift. We drove the kids to their jobs and loaned it to families for job interviews and vacations. We even taught kids how to drive in it. Many amazing moments of ministry took place in that minivan. Because of the generosity of our friends, we got a beautiful taste of the age to come.

I often reflect on the kind of generosity that God unleashed through this couple. Rather than hoarding possessions for themselves, they gave their best to others. When I later asked my friend how he felt when giving us the van, he said, "It brought us incredible joy. It truly is better to give than to receive."

John the apostle put it like this:

> We know that we have passed from death to life, because we love each other. . . . This is how we know what love is: Jesus Christ laid down his life for us. And we ought to lay down our lives for our brothers and sisters. If anyone has material possessions and sees a brother or sister in need but has no pity on them, how can the love of God be in that person? Dear children, let us not love with words or speech but with actions and in truth.[12]

The resurrection of Jesus did not only happen so we could have a private theology, private piety, or private worship. It flows out to those around us. It's an economy of freedom: people giving out of liberated hearts, free from the curse of thinking this life is all there is. It's an economy of love that moves and acts and responds in the same way Jesus did for us. And this economy changes lives.

Why Do You Give?

The third thing Jesus does to break us out of the cycle of overconsumption is to transform our hearts. Some people have no use for the church because they think it exists to guilt people out of money. But Jesus never used guilt as a motivator. Guilt is so limited in its ability to effect change. Consider what giving out of guilt is like.

Giving under guilt cannot sustain generosity. It responds to a singular need. Giving out of guilt doesn't change us into generous people. It only asks the question, "How much do I have to give so that I won't feel like this anymore?" Giving out of guilt doesn't transform our hearts; it just makes us ask, "How low does the standard of my life need to be in order to appease my conscience?"

Rather than motivating by guilt, God's heart is that love will compel us. The Scriptures teach: "If I give all I possess to the poor, . . . but do not have love, I gain nothing."[13]

Our response to the needs of the world around us is based on what God has done for us in Christ. "For you know the grace of our Lord Jesus Christ, that though he was rich, yet for your sake he became poor, so that you through his poverty might become rich."[14] Our giving is to reflect Christ, who gave of his riches to lift us from the poverty of our souls.

Giving under guilt is reactive and sporadic. It does not flow out of a liberated heart but gives only for the moment, without touching our lifestyle. On the other hand, giving out of grace is proactive and intentional.* It is concerned with the ongoing stewardship and increasing the investment of our time, heart, and resources on behalf of others.

I (Jon) have a friend named Seth who works on Wall Street. He manages money well, but his real passion is what he calls his "eternal portfolio." He sees himself as a "spiritual venture capitalist." He strives to steward his earthly portfolio well so that he can transfer as much of it as possible to his eternal portfolio.

---

*I heard Tim Keller say this at a mentoring meeting I was a part of.

Whenever he sees an opportunity for the kingdom of God to advance, he helps fund it. Whenever he sees a practical need, he helps meet it. Whenever there are planning meetings about the future of the church, he wants to speak into it so we can think about the long-term impacts of stewarding kingdom capital. He is literally walking around looking for ways to give his money to needs in the community and to expand the kingdom. Even though the amount he gives is often not sizable from a financial standpoint, Seth is one of the most liberated people I know. His giving is consistent and thoughtful, and he has a growing portfolio in the kingdom of God because of how he has stewarded his life.

THE GREAT REVERSAL

The United States is a spiritually dangerous place to live. We live in a society where we are assaulted by messages that urge us to consume and accumulate. These often compete for our affection and loyalty. Jesus gave a severe warning when he said:

> "Watch out! Be on your guard against all kinds of greed; life does not consist in an abundance of possessions." And he told them this parable: "The ground of a certain rich man yielded an abundant harvest. He thought to himself, 'What shall I do? I have no place to store my crops.' Then he said, 'This is what I'll do. I will tear down my barns and build bigger ones, and there I will store my surplus grain. And I'll say to myself, 'You have plenty of grain laid up for many years. Take life easy; eat, drink and be merry.'

"But God said to him, 'You fool! This very night your life will be demanded from you. Then who will get what you have prepared for yourself?'

"This is how it will be with whoever stores up things for themselves but is not rich toward God."[15]

Paul said, "To live is Christ and to die is gain."[16] This is the compelling vision of a life centered on the beauty and mission of Jesus—the eternal portfolio.

Living in a consumer culture reverses the biblical vision: "To live is gain and to die is Christ." It is a quiet subversion of the meaning and purpose of our lives. Accumulate as much as you can. Build bigger barns, then take life easy—eat, drink, and be merry. After enjoying the benefits of indulgent living, when you die you go to be with Christ. The great tragedy of materialistic America is not financial abundance, but spiritual poverty.

Jesus wants to save us from giving our lives to things that just don't matter. In a culture that relentlessly reminds us of what we don't have—the "silver medal syndrome"—the Scriptures bring blinding illumination. Life does not consist in an abundance of possessions. Do not put your hope in wealth. Put your hope in God, be rich in good deeds, be generous and willing to share. In doing so you will take hold of the life that is truly life.[17]

Growing up, Brad shared a small house with many siblings. The poverty that defined his childhood instilled a determination to make a better life. As a teenager he showed an early drive to be successful. He worked longer and harder than his peers, and by the time he was in his late twenties he had made his first million dollars. He enjoyed the lifestyle and comforts that this level of success afforded him, but he often felt hollow and empty. He continued this financially successful trajectory into several business ventures over the next ten years.

One day someone invited him to our (Jon's) church, and he encountered Jesus. Over the next year he wrestled with the implications of the Scripture's challenge to the rich. One day as he was driving down the interstate in his Ferrari, he looked at the Rolex on his wrist and thought, *After all this success, I still feel like something is missing.* With Jesus' words echoing in his mind he made a radical decision. He contacted a small nonprofit ministry that serves homeless single mothers and told them he wanted to donate a few items. Brad donated his Ferrari, his Rolex, and several other expensive items of jewelry. Brad is taking hold of the life that is truly life.

Jillian is a doctor who works in the city. She learned that the man who lived next door to her had recently lost his job. He was the sole income provider for his small family. For more than a year she watched him struggle to find another job and witnessed this family descend into financial ruin. One day she discovered that her neighbor's home was facing foreclosure. On the same day she was offered an extra shift at the hospital. Somehow she felt these two events were connected. She committed to the extra shift each month and started to make the monthly payment on her neighbor's home. Even when she's exhausted, Jillian's favorite overtime shift is the one where all the money she earns goes toward paying her neighbor's mortgage. Jillian is taking hold of the life that is truly life.

Mark and Carol are a married couple who own a small printing business. They were once crippled by credit card debt. After fifteen years paying off credits cards, they are now debt free. Today they have established a fund that is available for single mothers who are wrestling with debt, with a dollar-for-dollar matching program. As they retire these long-term debts these moms feel the collective momentum of the generosity of others. Mark and Carol are taking hold of the life that is truly life.

Peter and Alison met Nate at their son's school. The first thing anyone noticed about Nate was his teeth. Nate was very self-conscious about his smile. For as long as he could remember, other kids had mocked him for his extremely crooked teeth. His single mom lacked the resources to do anything about it. Moved with compassion, Peter and Alison organized and are paying for three years of orthodontic treatment for Nate. Peter and Alison are taking hold of the life that is truly life.

In an economic climate like ours, the world is wondering if the rumors of a generous God are true. The church is the place where God wants to confirm the truth of these rumors. May it be said of us as it was of the early church:

> They love one another. . . . And he, who has, gives to him who has not, without boasting. And when they see a stranger, they take him in to their own homes and rejoice over him as a very brother. . . . And if there is among them any that is poor and needy, and if they have no spare food, they fast two or three days in order to supply to the needy their lack of food. . . . Such, O King, is their manner of life. . . . And verily, this is a new people, and there is something divine in the midst of them.[18]
>
> —Aristides to the Caesar Hadrian

May Christ be our gain and may we take hold of the life that is truly life.

CHAPTER FOUR

THE FAITH YOU'VE ONLY HEARD ABOUT

Rumors of Love

We love him, because he first loved us.

—John, the beloved disciple

Have you been loved well by someone? So well that you feel confident that person will receive you and will forgive your worst crime? That's the kind of security the soul receives from God. When the soul lives in that kind of security, it is no longer occupied with technique. We can go back and do the rituals, the spiritual disciplines, but we no longer follow them idolatrously. We don't condemn people who don't do it our way. All techniques, rituals and spiritual disciplines are just fingers pointing to God. God is the important thing, not the pointing fingers.

—Richard Rohr, *Everything Belongs*

Those who say that they believe in God and yet neither love nor fear him, do not in fact believe in him, but in those who have taught them that God exists. Those who believe that they believe in God, but without any passion in their heart, any anguish of mind, without uncertainty, without doubt, without an element of despair even in their consolation, believe only in the God-idea, not in God.

—Miguel de Unamuno

When I (Jon) first became a Christian I was dumbfounded by the love of God. It was overwhelming. It was everything. It was a total surprise. I wasn't looking to become a Christian. I wasn't even remotely interested in God. I starting dating a girl who attended a local youth group and she strongly encouraged me to come along. I stumbled into the basement of a church literally called Paradise and was in disbelief at what I encountered.

Hundreds of people were crying out and worshiping God with a passion and intensity I had never seen in my life. I was repelled and attracted at the same time. I was scared of becoming a religious fanatic, but drawn to the passion I sensed in their midst. During a period of about eight months, my heart began to soften, and I found myself encountering the source of their passion: Jesus.

Love drew me to Jesus. I was stunned that he didn't seem to want to manipulate or condemn me or regulate my behavior to external laws. He seemed to be after something else. *Me.* This revelation, and my response to it, completely altered the passion, vision, and direction of my life.

At the time this new relationship with Jesus took over my life,

I was a recent high school dropout working as a butcher at a meat wholesaler. Jesus spoke so strongly to me—his presence so unbelievably tangible—I would often weep while standing in a meat freezer filled with carcasses. The Holy Spirit would speak to me through the Scriptures I was memorizing. Even as I was working a seemingly insignificant job, I could feel my life being swept into something far greater than I had ever imagined. I used to drive back to church during my lunch break and spend that hour seeking the face of God.

Darren started attending the same church. We decided to get up at 4:00 a.m. every day and drive to the parking lot of our church to seek God before work. We couldn't wait for the Sunday worship service—we had to meet and pray and be with God. Literally, we couldn't get enough.

I had a growing conviction that the love of God was too great to keep from people, so the location of the 4:00 a.m. prayer meeting changed. We headed to the center of our city, to a place called Rundle Mall, and would spend the early hours of the day crying out for God to shower his love on our city. We took Communion on our knees and prayed for a revelation of love to cover the place.

At this point there was nothing mixed about our motives. It was love: for God, from God, and a desire for others to experience this love that had so transformed us.

This same passion is what ultimately led us to the United States. We wanted to be part of an awakening of the kingdom of God in our time. We wanted people to encounter Jesus and the kingdom he was bringing to earth, and we wanted to go to places of influence and make a difference. We were trying to perform cultural acupuncture, to touch the nerve centers of the world, so the ripple effect of God's love would be felt to the ends of the earth.

Within six months of each other, we packed our lives into a couple of suitcases and headed to the United States.

RUMORS OF PASSION

When I landed here in America, I understood little about church growth, church programming, church leadership, outreach strategies, cultural conflicts, being relevant, contextualization, or much else for that matter. But I did understand that the Scriptures were rooted and grounded in the love of Christ. So I kept getting up early and seeking the face of God. Slowly people began to tell me that living my life like this was unsustainable.

I explained that in the book of Acts the believers met daily, cried out to God in prayer, and that the grace of God was powerfully at work in their midst. Generosity flowed from their hearts and there were no needy people among them. The city was in awe at the grace of God poured out upon those early believers. Some people reminded me that I wasn't in the book of Acts, I was in America, so I needed to calm it down. Undiscouraged, I was intent in my soul to keep my passion for Jesus alive at any cost.

FAST-FORWARD TEN YEARS

Darren is working as a teaching pastor at one of the largest churches in America, and I am helping plant a network of churches in America's largest city. We came to the United States and ended up in places with real potential for impact, but something was missing. Late one night we chatted on the phone about

God's kindness in bringing us to our current ministries. But there was also a deep sense of sadness in our hearts. Maybe the critics were right. America is definitely not the book of Acts.

Somehow the pressures and stress and distraction and struggles and planning and cares and critics had slowly won us over. We were in positions of influence, good things were happening; but we'd lost something along the way.

We'd lost our passion for Jesus—the very person who brought us here in the first place.

EXCHANGING PASSION FOR DUTY

Have you ever burned with a passion for God that was contagious? Or felt as if the only thing that mattered in life was walking with God and living in his presence? Was there a time when church was a privilege, worship an encounter, the Bible rich, and witnessing effortless? How would you describe your heart now?

Where did all the passion go?

Trying to figure out what it takes to sustain a passionate walk with God is tough. We go to church looking for life, yet often find it disappointing and shallow. We do our devotions, yet it feels more like duty. We share our faith if it happens to come up but wonder if the message is even true. While going through a similar season, author Donald Miller expressed it like this: "I have become an infomercial for God, and I don't even use the product."[1]

How do we go about sustaining passion for Jesus in the midst of a world like ours? How do we transform what we know to be true about God into a passionate reality, into a vibrant love for Jesus that burns with intensity?

MORE THAN GOOD

While teaching through a series in Revelation, I was struck by what Jesus said about the church of Ephesus. The passage is a microstory about a community that started with passion for Jesus but settled for faithfulness. The more I studied, the more I realized how understanding this ancient church could help us reclaim our passion for God.

The Ephesian Christians' experience paralleled my own in so many ways. Though our cultures are separated by almost two thousand years, they are eerily similar. Ephesus was a city dominated by a Greek goddess named Artemis. Originally believed to have fallen from heaven, a statue of her was enshrined in a magnificent temple, one of the Seven Wonders of the World. The city was defined by her presence: The industry, economy, community, family, calendar, social, and religious landscape all fell under her shadow.

Into this dominant cultural narrative, the apostle Paul proclaimed the good news of Jesus Christ. The response in the city was incredible. People repented and believed, the church was established, and a new cultural narrative filled the city—the story of Jesus. From the beginning, the church seemed to be headed in the right direction. Jesus started by commending the church for the things they were doing right—things most of us are diligent to pay attention to in our own lives.

The first thing he commended was their endurance. "I know your deeds," said Jesus, "your hard work and your perseverance."[2] Some of the early Christians had begun to feel a backlash from the Roman Empire. Christianity was finally recognized as its own religion apart from Judaism, and the Romans viewed it as a threat. But in spite of imperial hostility, the church persevered.

Many of us feel similar opposition today. Increasingly secular, our culture often mocks Christians for being judgmental and narrow-minded. Jesus loves that we persevere in the midst of this.

Jesus also loved that the Ephesian Christians valued holiness. In Ephesus, pagan worship often involved sexual immorality. The temple prostitutes would offer their bodies as living sacrifices to Artemis; they would invite the spirit of the goddess to come and inhabit their bodies. The way you "met the goddess" was to have sex with a prostitute who had the spirit of Artemis in her. As you were together, your spirit would mingle with the spirit of Artemis.

Imagine living in such a culture. Because these Christians remained holy in the face of such egregious immorality, they found favor with Jesus. They were careful not to allow the values and culture of the city to creep into the church—they were a distinct people. We feel this same push in our time: declining morality, cheapening sexuality, greed, lust, and violence are becoming the normal way of life. When we resist these things and reserve our lives as places of worship for the living God, it pleases his heart. Jesus loves this about the church.

The next thing Jesus commended was their doctrine. Ephesus was an important travel destination, and people from all over the world brought new religious ideas and philosophies. People were often drawn to these new teachings and the exciting communities they formed. Earlier in Acts, Paul warned the Ephesian elders that even from among their own number false teachers would arise and distort the faith. The Ephesians guarded their doctrine and resisted false apostles.

We are inundated with theological options in our world. Books, blogs, sermons, and podcasts clutter our thoughts and minds. With so much information at our fingertips it's paramount that we are more diligent than ever to make sure that our beliefs are rooted in Scripture and the historic orthodox faith. And Jesus loves this. He loves when people see him clearly and worship him in truth.

Finally, Jesus commended the Ephesians for their hard work. The Ephesian Christian community busied themselves with missions, seeing the gospel expand in Asia Minor and beyond. These early believers were not defined by spiritual laziness.

Likewise, the American church seems more industrious than ever. We are often the first to roll up our sleeves and join God in his great restorative work of our time. Jesus loves that we want to be about his Father's business.

When I stop to reflect on the kind of church Jesus saw at Ephesus, I can see why there was a lot to commend. People were defined by faithful perseverance, holiness, correct doctrine, and diligent hard work. What else could Jesus possibly want from them?

"Yet I hold this against you," Jesus said. "You have forsaken the love you had at first. Consider how far you have fallen!"[3]

Imagine receiving this letter and hearing it read before the congregation. Everyone's nodding in agreement, congratulating one another for their commendations. And then the bishop reads this line. It cuts to the core. But it reveals something special about Jesus' heart: he cares most for people, for his family members— his bride. He wants more than a life lived *for* him. He wants us to live *with* him—a people defined not by what we do but by *whose we are*. As in all love stories, if you don't cultivate the original romance, eventually it will cool.

Somehow, in the midst of all the responsibilities of my life, I had forsaken the love I had at first. I was no longer up early, seeking God's face in the morning; I was heading straight to the office to build God's kingdom. Yes, I was still spending time with God, and the church I was pastoring had many commendable elements, but I sensed that like the church in Ephesus, maybe Jesus had something against us too. We had forsaken our first love.

RUMORS OF PASSION

So what does it take to remain passionately in love with Jesus? What do you think it takes to keep an individual life and a community of believers filled with the love and life of God?

Many of us wrestle with this question daily. We get excited about a new teaching series or speaker, a new campaign, a worship CD, or a church. Yet every time the initial excitement fades away. I think many people today fall into the quick-fix trap—like an "Easy button" for enlivening our passion for God.

Here are the most common traps I think people fall into regarding sustaining love for God.

The SuperPastor

We live in the age of the celebrity pastor. Church leaders think that if they can get the right pastor in their church, then he or she will singlehandedly be able to keep their passion hot. We rely on the pastor's teaching, the programs they bring to the table, the worship leaders they can attract, and the insight they have on the Scriptures to enflame our hearts. When the pastor is doing well, we feel great; but when they struggle, we hate it. We either look for the next SuperPastor or go to another church where there is one.

The church at Ephesus had a stunning string of leaders. The

apostle Paul founded the church, his disciple Timothy followed him,[4] and then the apostle John was the leader of the church.[5] May I make a humble suggestion here? If the leadership and teaching of the apostle Paul, his disciple Timothy, and the apostle John were not enough to sustain passion in the Ephesian church, there is not another man or woman alive today who can sustain ours on our behalf. A SuperPastor is not the solution for sustaining passion for God.

The Miraculous

Often we can fall into the trap of thinking that if we could see more of God's miraculous power in our lives, then we would remain in love with God. Not so simple. When the church at Ephesus was founded, "God did extraordinary miracles through Paul, so that even handkerchiefs and aprons that had touched him were taken to the sick, and their illnesses were cured and the evil spirits left them."[6]

Can you imagine how extraordinary that would be? People were healed and demons were cast out without the leader even being present. Imagine bringing a napkin that your pastor had touched to your workplace and people watching it heal and deliver those who touched it. You'd think such power would have to keep them in love with God. Not so. Forty years later, despite the miraculous, the Christians at Ephesus had lost their spiritual fervor. As much as I crave the reality of God's power in my life, it's not the final solution to sustaining spiritual passion.

Cultural Impact

"Cultural renewal" is one of the rallying themes of our day. We often hear, for example, "The reason no one cares about God is because he is no longer the center of our culture. If we could just make an impact in our culture, and invade Hollywood and Wall Street with Christian truth, then people would see Jesus in all of life and love him."

As valuable as cultural impact is, it still does not guarantee passion for God. Look what happened when the Ephesian church was started:

> When this became known to the Jews and Greeks living in Ephesus, they were all seized with fear, and the name of the Lord Jesus was held in high honor. Many of those who believed now came and openly confessed what they had done. A number who had practiced sorcery brought their scrolls together and burned them publicly. When they calculated the value of the scrolls, the total came to fifty thousand drachmas. In this way the word of the Lord spread widely and grew in power.[7]

Imagine large-scale public confession in your city. People burning occult books in public bonfires. Imagine the word of the Lord spreading widely and growing in power. A stunning cultural impact! Surely such dynamic cultural influence would be enough to keep the church in love with God. Not so. Forty years later, the church at Ephesus had still forsaken its first love.

Mission

I often hear people say, "We don't love God because we don't love what he loves." We're selfish and inwardly focused. We need to recover the *Missio Dei*, the mission of God. When we are swept into the mission of God, then we will recover our love for God.

The Ephesian church had a missional vision:

> Paul entered the synagogue and spoke boldly there for
> three months, arguing persuasively about the kingdom of
> God. But some of them became obstinate; they refused to
> believe and publicly maligned the Way. So Paul left them.
> He took the disciples with him and had discussions daily in
> the lecture hall of Tyrannus. This went on for two years,
> so that all the Jews and Greeks who lived in the province
> of Asia heard the word of the Lord.[8]

Paul gathered the interested disciples and spent two years
pouring into them. They forged a vision for their region, went
out, planted churches, and then *the entire region* heard the word of
the Lord. Imagine if a small community of people reached more
than their city—their entire *region*. In two years? Staggering! Yet
even this missional vision did not sustain passion for Jesus. The
Ephesian church still lost its first love.

If godly leadership, the miraculous power of God, impacting
our culture, discipleship, and outward focused evangelism were
not enough to keep the Ephesians from forsaking their first love,
then why do we think we are different?

I am convinced that we've fallen into the trap of thinking the
things of God are sacred substitutes for God himself.

REMEMBER THE HEIGHTS

We need to regain our heavenly perspective.

Paul told the Ephesians that they were seated with Christ in the heavenly places.[9] And so are we. We are called to live from the perspective of a high and holy union with Christ. But, invariably, we take this for granted and drop back to an earthly perspective, the normal grunt and grind of doing things for God. We end up relegating the church to a mere organization, while our union with God falls to the theoretical. We forget the wonder of our identity and position in Christ.

We live in a world that suffers from amnesia. We are so bombarded with marketing and noise and products and distractions that we often forget to *whom* we belong. Stripped of wonder and mystery, our ministry work hobbles onward—a busy, holy, theologically correct, passionless faith.

But God does not desire the things we can do for him. God desires fellowship with us. How do we return to this foundational truth? Jesus said to the Ephesians, "Repent and do the things you did at first. If you do not repent, I will come to you and remove your lampstand from its place."[10] The repentance Jesus spoke of includes the elimination of sin *and* the restoration of our hearts. God does not want religious duty and obligation; he wants us to respond to him with gratitude and love.

Paul taught that Christians should live their lives rooted in the love of God. Our roots, our thriving, and our passion all draw their nourishment from the love the Father has poured out on us in Christ. Paul wrote: "I pray that you, being rooted and established in love, may have power, together with all the Lord's holy people, to grasp how wide and long and high and deep is the love of Christ, and to know this love that surpasses knowledge—that you may be filled to the measure of all the fullness of God."[11]

A faith based on performance is antithetical to the gospel. We are loved because of what Christ has done for us. It's all about him. The primary job of the Christian life is to remain in how God feels about us, not how we feel about him.

AN INDIFFERENT BRIDE

So how do we obey Jesus? How do we remain in his great love for us? I think the first thing we have to do is value the voice of Jesus above everything else. Our culture conspires to pull us away from sincere and simple devotion to Christ. We must commit to making the voice of Jesus the loudest voice in our lives.

While studying the Gospels, I spent some time meditating on the baptism of Jesus, to see how he remained in his Father's love. Jesus' baptism is one of the most insightful moments in the Gospels. It's like overhearing a conversation between the Trinity: "As soon as Jesus was baptized, he went up out of the water. At that moment heaven was opened, and he saw the Spirit of God descending like a dove and alighting on him. And a voice from heaven said, 'This is my Son, whom I love; with him I am well pleased.' "[12]

I had never before noticed the timing of this verse in Jesus' life. Jesus was yet to cast out demons, raise the dead, confront the Pharisees, train his disciples, die for our sins, or be resurrected from the grave; yet, the Father tells him that he is pleased with him. Jesus, until this point, had been laboring in obscurity as a humble carpenter; so what was the Father pleased with? It couldn't have been his ministry or his teaching or his leadership, as these were yet to happen. What had Jesus done that made the Father proud? He had spent thirty years cultivating an abiding passion and love for God. The only glimpse we have of Jesus in his early years is in the temple, seeking to be about his Father's business.

Could it be that God is most pleased not with what we do for him but with the life of love we cultivate with him? Maybe this is why Jesus seemed so free from needing the approval of men. He had all the approval he needed; the voice of his Father drowned out the voice of the crowd. I began to see that if I were going to live a life that was truly pleasing to God, my primary task would have to shift from doing things for God to living life with him. What I had forgotten about the early years of my faith was the thing that had captured my life—not getting to serve God in ministry—but serving God himself. I began to see that the primary task of my life was to prioritize time with God and learn to hear his blessing and love spoken over me. Only then would I be free from the crowd and the addiction to accomplishments.

We need to learn how to *receive* God's love. This proves difficult for many of us. It's important we realize that anything we do out of love for God is a response to his great love for us. I no longer rush off to the office first thing. I set the alarm, get up early, and seek God's face. But I don't do it out of shame and guilt. I do it out of passion. I open his Word to the wonder of his truth and promises and slowly let them flood my soul. I drink in his unconditional love. I meditate slowly and intentionally through the passages of Scripture that talk about who God is and how he feels about me—his grace and beauty and peace and love.

When I was studying Ephesians, I saw that Jesus desires a glorious church, one without spot or blemish or any such thing. He wants the truth of his Word and the flow of his Spirit to wash over my life and remove the sin and stain so I am ready for him. I love beginning each day knowing that I am a child of God, dearly loved.

After I have drunk deeply from the fountain of God's love, I listen to what God is asking from me. I want to respond in obedience to exactly what it is that he wants me to do. It's so easy to fill our lives with good programs and people. The needs of our day are often overwhelming. If I'm not careful, I get into the trap of responding to everything in front of me, instead of listening to what the Father is asking of me. We are responsible to respond to what God puts in our hearts and serve him faithfully in that first.

I recently attended the wedding of one of my closest friends. It was an incredible day. The highlight of the event was the moment the doors opened and the bride appeared. The bride and the groom spontaneously started weeping (as did the whole room). It was such a powerful reflection of Christ as the Bridegroom and his bride the church.

But it got me thinking. What would have happened if the doors opened and the groom began weeping while the bride remained indifferent? What if she whispered to her father walking her down the aisle, "We might as well get on with it so we can have kids and a family and a nice little house." Everyone would stop and shout, "Don't do it! Marriage is designed for a couple who is insatiably in love."

Are we the indifferent bride? What is your attitude as part of the bride of Christ to the Groom?

May God give us all the grace to receive and respond, to position ourselves to see his immeasurable love spill into our lives in unimaginable ways. May we all experience not just the rumors of passion, but its overflowing reality as we remain in his love.

"Now to him who is able to do immeasurably more than all we ask or imagine, according to his power that is at work within us, to him be glory in the church and in Christ Jesus throughout all generations, for ever and ever! Amen."[13]

CHAPTER FIVE

— GETTING THE GOSPEL IN ORDER —

Rumors of Grace

Questioner to Billy Graham: "Why are you here sup-
porting President Clinton after everything he has
done?"
Billy Graham's reply: "It is the Holy Spirit's job to con-
vict, God's job to judge, and it's my job to love."

*The law was brought in so that the trespass might increase.
But where sin increased, grace increased all the more, so that,
just as sin reigned in death, so also grace might reign through
righteousness to bring eternal life through Jesus Christ our Lord.*

—St. Paul to the church in Rome

Perhaps you are familiar with the following story.

Several people were debating the difference between major
religions. After much discussion, C. S. Lewis walked into

the room and they asked him, "What is the major difference between Christianity and other religions?"

"That's simple," he replied. "It's grace." And then he left the room.

Simple, grace.

If you were to ask people today what the major difference is between Christianity and other faiths, I think people would reply, "That's simple. Christians are judgmental."

Simple, judgmental.

YOU WILL KNOW THEM FOR THEIR JUDGMENT

While I (Jon) was in Bible college, I worked in the meat department of a small supermarket in Texas. One of my coworkers on the evening shift was a young woman, and we seemed to get along quite well at first. Then one night I saw her kissing another girl outside the back of the store. Knowing I was a Christian, she pulled me aside later and said, "You must hate me now that you know I'm gay."

"Why?" I asked.

"Because you're a Christian, and all Christians hate gay people."

Her statement took me aback. Of all the things that are taught in Scripture, how is it that the one thing she was able to discern about Jesus was that his followers hate gay people? How did the beauty and mystery and richness of the gospel get reduced to that? It seems that this "simple grace" has been hidden under an insurmountable pile of religious and cultural baggage. The good news—that Jesus was a friend of sinners—has been lost in our time.

It breaks my heart that Christians are not defined by the scandalous grace of Jesus. Grace is a hallmark of Jesus' ministry. I'm moved by his encounters with people: the woman at the well, his calling of Matthew the tax collector, his dinner with Zacchaeus, his tenderness toward the woman who washed his feet with her tears, his rebuke of the heartless Pharisees through the parable of the prodigal son, and the kindness he showed to the woman caught in adultery. Where are these kinds of encounters in our lives today?

I recently walked through a group of Christians protesting a parade that was making its way through the neighborhood where our church is located. One of the people in the parade yelled back at the protestors, "Aren't you supposed to be defined by love? Where is your grace?"

The service that evening went particularly well, but no matter how many times I heard "Good sermon!" I couldn't shake the challenge from the parade: "Aren't you supposed to be defined by love? Where is your grace?"

I had a nagging sense that our church was not demonstrating the beauty of this grace. Were we just a community of decent people who loved to gather and worship, or was our community defined by the love and grace of God? This challenge is not a general challenge to a group of Christians, but a personal challenge to you and to me. If you were to ask the people who know you best, would they say that love and grace accurately describe who you've become? Or would they ask, "Where is your grace?" Would they be pondering, "Aren't you supposed to be defined by love?"

If we are going to transform these rumors of grace into powerful encounters with its reality, we need to reexamine our approach to sin, judgment, the gospel, and truth.

RECOVERING OUR NEED FOR GRACE

Grace exists to deal with our rebellion and the horror of the fall. But in spite of sin's reality, we are called to anchor our message in the fact that Christ came not to condemn the world, but to save it. Jesus said he did not come to call the righteous but to call sinners to repentance and that there is more joy in heaven over one sinner who repents than over ninety-nine righteous people who do not need to.[1]

So how do we prove the rumor of God's grace to be true in the midst of our depravity? How do we become a people who are defined by the unique message Jesus offers? Let's start by looking at the condition of sin that grace works so powerfully to redeem.

Sin

I don't know of a place in the Scriptures that describes our need for grace more clearly than the second chapter of Ephesians. Paul was writing to people who lived in a thoroughly godless context when he penned the following words:

> As for you, you were dead in your transgressions and sins, in which you used to live when you followed the ways of this world and of the ruler of the kingdom of the air, the spirit who is now at work in those who are disobedient. All of us also lived among them at one time, gratifying the cravings of our sinful nature and following its desires and thoughts. Like the rest, we were by nature deserving of wrath.[2]

Contrary to popular belief, the Scriptures teach that our essential nature is rebellion against God rather than essential goodness and virtue. I know that this can sound like a harsh judgment, particularly since we live in a culture that seems so spiritual. You might ask, "How can it be that there are so many people who are so loving and kind but are not followers of Jesus?" The Scriptures don't teach that we have lost the image of God due to our sin. They teach that we've lost our spiritual capacity to rightly relate to God. And so we can still do things of real beauty, and we are still capable of kindness, but not because we are spiritually good. It's because we're made in the image of God, and the traces of that image didn't disappear when we fell.

We have lost our hearts, our spiritual capacity for communion with God. God is a spirit, and our dead hearts live alienated from him. It's like a home after a couple has divorced: the home is still physically there and may be filled with beautiful things, but the relationship it was founded upon is gone. The house, though physically present, is relationally dead.

These verses from Ephesians teach that we are like that: our lives remain filled with many beautiful things from God, but the founding relationship has died. We are still in our home, but God's presence and life have gone. This is why Paul, earlier in Ephesians, prayed for spiritual enlightenment.[3] We are wise in many areas of our lives—our finances, our careers, our opinions—yet when it comes to the state of our souls, without Christ we are in the dark.

Controlled

We next see that our lives are *controlled* by our sinful nature. Our sinful nature isn't an occasional temptation; it's the defining influence in our lives. It's the core motivation, our deepest instinct, our primal response to all we are and do.

We were created to live with dignity and honor. We were

made to represent God in the world and rule over it. But when sin corrupts us, we end up living like animals, ruled by our instincts.

People crave others sexually, so they sleep with them.

People crave food, so they overeat.

People crave luxury, so they spend.

People crave power, so they manipulate.

We are confused about what it means to be human and often end up living by these base instincts. Animals don't enter into deep reflection about the moral, spiritual and ethical ramifications of their behavior; they just act according to instinct. Paul was declaring that in our spiritual deadness we stop acting out of consideration for God and simply follow our desires wherever they lead. Try this simple experiment:

Try never being mean to anyone again.

Try never being selfish again.

Try to eat healthy for the rest of your life.

Try never judging others in your mind.

How long do you think you would last? C. S. Lewis once commented that no one knows how truly bad he is until he has tried very hard to be good.

Enslaved

We are spiritually dead and controlled by our sinful nature, and we cannot break free. Paul described this as *enslavement*. We are in bondage to the sinfulness within ourselves, which is what the Scriptures call *the flesh*. When we talk about the flesh, we usually assume it means our physical bodies. Christians have stereotypically thought of sins of the flesh as sexual sins. But this is an inadequate understanding. The flesh is more accurately described as the systems, strategies, and structures we create to live without God. Those attitudes, habits, and desires serve as functional gods in our lives, the things we do to keep us from depending on God, the things that reinforce our autonomy in the world.

Most Christians probably think, *Thank goodness I'm not like that. I haven't committed any major sins, so I'm not enslaved to the flesh.* But if you pay close attention, you will see this in the church all the time. People use religion as a coping mechanism for life apart from God. It's the sinful nature at work, with "Service for God" painted over the top.

Have you ever been in a small group led by a manipulative and controlling leader? The leader might have been using the group to avoid humbling himself or herself before God, and it results in manipulation. Have you ever met people who do incredible justice work but are critical and judgmental of others who don't exhibit the same concern for the poor and less fortunate? They may have been using their service to keep from dealing with issues in their own hearts. Paul said we have all been enslaved by our sinful nature—sinners and saints—and we do not possess the awareness or ability to do anything about it. It's a heartbreaking truth: we are slaves to ourselves.

FROM PEOPLE TO STATUES

We find ourselves in a hopeless condition. God created us with his life pulsating through our veins, walking in close communion with him. There was a rumor circulating in the garden of Eden that disobedience would bring death, and it turns out it was true. When we disobeyed, we were transformed from people back into statues, devoid of the life of God, spiritually dead, enslaved to sin, children of wrath, born into a system we could not escape, taken hostage to do the devil's will, and unable to free ourselves. As a result of living like this, our lives are absolutely riddled with pain, shame, regret, and remorse.

Look at our world. Look at your world. The proof is in our hearts. We know deep in our souls that we've been separated from God, and that we cannot change ourselves. Our lives are filled with coping mechanisms to keep us from depending on God.[4] We continually fall short of our own expectations, and we are haunted by the reality that this is not all we were created to be.

Instead of God asking us to fix this mess ourselves, he steps in and acts decisively on our behalf. In the middle of our rebellion, sin, and depravity, God saves us. Paul put it like this:

> But because of his great love for us, God, who is rich in mercy, made us alive with Christ even when we were dead in transgressions—it is by grace you have been saved. And God raised us up with Christ and seated us with him in the heavenly realms in Christ Jesus, in order that in the coming ages he might show the incomparable riches of his grace, expressed in his kindness to us in Christ Jesus. For it is by grace you have been saved, through faith—and this

is not from yourselves, it is the gift of God—not by works, so that no one can boast.[5]

Knowing that we were steeped in sin and facing separation from God physically, spiritually, and eternally, and that we could do nothing to save ourselves, Jesus entered human history as our perfect substitute. He communicated God's love for us and did what we could not do for ourselves. He was born of a virgin and lived a perfect, sinless life of submission to his Father. He lived the life we could not live.

Jesus allowed himself to be arrested and tried, and on the cross, God the Father took our sin—past, present, and future—and put it on Jesus and punished him in our place. Three days later, Jesus rose from the dead, proving sin no longer had a hold on him. He now invites us to turn away from our sin, to him, and to receive eternal life in his name.

Instead of having to pay for our sins, he gives us his life, his righteousness, and his standing. This stunning grace is the Rosetta stone of understanding the gospel.

GRACE

It's been my experience that Christians often confuse grace and mercy. The following is a common example.

Imagine you are driving down the interstate, doing 110 mph in a 55-mph zone. All of a sudden you see flashing lights, and a highway patrol officer pulls you over. You have been caught in the act. When the officer comes up to the window, he asks, "Sir, do you know how fast you were going?"

You answer, "Crickey mate, I had no idea." Your Australian accent seems to be of no avail. The officer pulls out his ticket book, so you start to pray. "Dear God. If you will get me off, just this once, I promise to finally enroll my tithe in automatic monthly debit."

Much to your surprise he says to you, "All right, I'm going to let you off."

Your body floods with joy. You drive home and tell your family, "I just experienced the grace of God through the highway patrol!"

The only problem with this illustration is that it's not an example of grace; it's an example of mercy. Most people think that simply being forgiven of our sins is an act of grace. But grace is much richer than that.

Imagine you're driving down the interstate and speeding again, but this time you've been drinking. The highway patrol officer pulls you over, and you know that you're guilty. You're dreading the consequences.

The officer comes up to you and asks, "Did you know that you were speeding? Have you been drinking?"

He gives you a Breathalyzer, and it confirms that you're over the legal limit.

To your surprise he responds, "Here's what's going to happen. I'm going to go to jail for you and take the penalty for your crimes." He hands you the keys to a brand-new BMW. Then he gives you the account information for his investments, which total twenty-four million dollars. He says, "I am going to trade identities with you so that I get punished and you get my inheritance."

This is more like what God has done for us in Jesus. We

deserve God's wrath and punishment, and yet he brings us into his kingdom. He adopts us as his sons and daughters. He gives us everything that Christ has and says that we will rule and reign with him. That's what grace is. That is good news. That's what God has done for us. All other religions are human attempts to reach God. Christianity is God coming for us. This is the wonder of the grace of God.

LOST IN TRANSLATION

How has this message gotten lost in translation? Why are we known as a people of hate, not a people of grace? One of the most interesting things about the Gospels is that Jesus rarely critiqued sinners. In fact, the people Jesus warned about hell were the religious people. Jesus said to sinners, "Are you thirsty? Do you want eternal life? Come and drink freely."

We often think our mission is to go into the world to condemn it. But the world is already condemned. Jesus came to offer the world his unparalleled grace. "God did not send his Son into the world to condemn the world, but through him to save the world."[6]

There is no doubt that we live in confusing times. Everything seems to be changing so quickly. As believers we find ourselves pushed to the fringe of our culture. In the midst of this confusion, we try to make sense of how we got here and to start challenging the evils that pushed us out, rather than declaring the truth that sets us free.

Some Christians believe our primary job is to decry the evils of postmodernism and recover absolute truth. Although absolute truth matters, Jesus' primary goal was to connect people to himself, not to theology. Others believe our primary task is good apologetics, to show people why we are right and they are wrong. Yet Jesus seemed uninterested in debate. In fact, Jesus often taught by asking questions in order to get people to think for themselves. Others believe our job is to confront immorality and the lapse of traditional values.

Because we spend our time fighting *against* things, nobody ends up knowing what we are *for*. Many people think that God hates their behavior and that they need to change in order for him to love them. For people steeped in sin, this feels like an impossible, crushing weight. Even Christians can get caught up in believing this is true about God. The message of grace gets buried under the obligations of moralism. When we make our central message anything other than the gospel of grace, we end up being known as a people of hate—judgmental, hypocritical, and defined by what we are against.

SALVATION REVISITED

In John chapter 8 we find the scene of the adulterous woman caught in the act by the Pharisees. It was just after dawn and they had brought her to Jesus. The Pharisees said, "Teacher, this woman was caught in the act of adultery. The law commands us to stone such women. Now what do you say?"

The Pharisees were attempting to trick Jesus so they could accuse him of wrongdoing. But Jesus bent down and started to write on the ground with his finger. Infuriated, the Pharisees pressed Jesus. "What do we do? She's *guilty!*"

The woman stood there as the crowd clutched rocks for

the stoning. Jesus continued finger-painting in the dust. Finally, he straightened up and said to them, "Let any one of you who is without sin be the first to throw a stone." Again he stooped down and wrote on the ground.

One by one, they dropped their stones and left, until only Jesus and the woman remained. Jesus asked, "Woman, where are they? Has no one condemned you?"

"No one, sir," she said.

"Then neither do I condemn you," Jesus declared. "Go now and leave your life of sin."

Curiously, Jesus didn't criticize the guilty woman. He didn't start pulling out the moral issues of the time. He didn't start talking about the divorce rate or how the institution of marriage was failing. He simply told the woman: "I don't condemn you. Now go and leave your life of sin."

In a guilty world riddled with immorality, who would you want to be with, the Pharisees or the person who showed you grace? Scripture says, "It is by grace we are saved, through faith."[7]

GETTING THE GOSPEL IN ORDER

It's hard to love our enemies. It's challenging to be kind to those who oppose our message. Often we fall into the trap of getting the gospel in the wrong order. We reverse it. We make it faith, then grace. We wait for people to think like us, act like us, believe like us, and behave like us; and when they do, we are kind to them. But this is not how the gospel works.

Scripture teaches that people are saved by grace through faith—they're not saved by faith through grace. I once heard a pastor say it like this: "Grace creates the conditions for faith; faith does not create the conditions for grace."[8] In other words, it is God's kindness toward us in the midst of our guilt that enables us to believe in him; it's not the expectation that once we believe in him, then he will be kind to us. God loved us when we were still his enemies, not once we have it all together.

The gay community hears the church say: "Change your ways, *then* God will love you." The Muslim community hears: "Change your ways, *then* we will love you." The atheist hears: "Believe in God, *then* he will love you." But what Jesus actually says is, "I love you now. As you are. Come to me. Receive my grace."

You don't have to change for God to love you. God loves you as you are. This is what enables you to change. Paul said: "God's kindness is intended to lead you to repentance."[9] It is not faith, then grace; it's grace, then faith.

LETTING GOD DEAL WITH OUR SIN

When my (Jon's) daughter was two years old, we were in an intense season of potty training. It seemed that everything my wife and I did as a married couple centered on helping our daughter to go to the bathroom by herself. About a week into this process, my wife felt that we were making enough progress to leave me to watch our daughter without her supervision. I took my daughter to Disney World in the morning, took her to lunch, to play, and around two o'clock we came home for her regular afternoon nap. Knowing my daughter was exhausted, I put a fresh diaper on her and popped her into her bed for a relaxing afternoon of rest.

I settled on the couch to do some light reading, when I was suddenly confronted with an overwhelming smell. At first I thought that the toilet had overflowed, so I got up and walked in to check. Nothing there. I walked all around the house to locate the source of it, when I suddenly realized the unthinkable had happened. Sure enough, I followed the smell toward my daughter's room. I braced myself to confront my failure as a parent.

When I opened the door the stench was overwhelming, but I couldn't see my daughter. What I could see, however, was some creative finger-painting done in interesting shades of green and brown, all over the walls. Her bed was empty except for the overflowing diaper that she had managed to pull off, and there were tiny brown footprints on the floor. I followed the prints to the wall, and then in a circle to find that they led back behind the door.

I found my tiny two-year-old daughter covered from head to toe with the smelly brown mess, with her tiny little hands over her face, whimpering in shame. I looked at the disaster of the room, and then back at her. How could someone so tiny make such a colossal mess? I suspected that, disappointed she had not used the potty, she slipped the dirty diaper off. As she did this, the mess got all over her. She tried wiping it off on the wall. Then she unknowingly stepped in the dirty diaper and left a trail around the room.

I knelt down to talk to her. "Sweetheart," I said. "What happened?"

She peeked through her hands, then burst into tears, held them up to me, and cried, "Pooooooh!"

I gently picked her up and walked with her into our bathroom. I couldn't find any bath soap, so I ended up using dishwashing detergent to wash her clean. The whole time she was crying, thinking she was in trouble. I tried to calm her down, but she refused to listen. Eventually I grabbed a giant white towel and gently dried her. I carried her downstairs, we sat on the couch, and she whimpered in my arms. I kept telling her that it was okay, she was not in trouble, and that Daddy would clean up all the mess. After about fifteen minutes my words finally sank in. She jumped out of the towel, ran and grabbed some toys, and then asked me if I wanted to play.

As I looked at this tiny little girl whom I loved with all my might, I pondered the idea of bringing our sin to God, instead of dealing with it on our own. So much of my daughter's shame was based on the fact that she tried to clean her mess herself, but she only ended up making things worse. God knows that we struggle. Christ himself is our advocate with the Father. Christ stands to acquit us based on his perfect work. Instead of trying to deal with our sexual failure, lies, bitterness, hatred, pride, and shame, we need to bring it all to Jesus. He will not only forgive our sin, but will cleanse us from all unrighteousness.[10]

Our world needs to know that the rumors of grace are true. There is a God who loves us in the midst of our rebellion, brokenness, and sin. He invites us to come freely to his throne to receive his grace and be transformed. God doesn't expect us to resurrect ourselves and restore our lives; it's a free gift he offers, and he is waiting to do it with joy. He is waiting to confirm that the rumors of grace are true.

CHAPTER SIX

GIVING UP YOUR RIGHTS

Rumors of Freedom

*I will never forgive the father who abdicated his moral and
legal responsibility to me and will never forgive someone else
for what they did to me. Neither of these people has ever asked
for or sought forgiveness. They are despicable human beings
and I have every right to hate them and to never forgive them.*

—Yvette, on a blog about forgiveness

*Every one says forgiveness is a lovely idea, until they have
something to forgive.*

—C. S. Lewis, *Mere Christianity*

*Bear with each other and forgive one another if any of you has
a grievance against someone. Forgive as the Lord forgave you.*

—St. Paul to the Colossians

T ell him to go to hell!"

Simon's sister was interested in reconnecting with their estranged father after more than a decade of absence. She asked her brother if there was anything he wanted her to communicate to their dad. "He abandoned and ignored us for our entire lives," Simon declared. "I wish him nothing but misery!" When Simon was two years old, his father left and his mother was on a downward spiral, addicted to heroin and alcohol. She lived much of her life in a catatonic state. Whether drunk or high, even when she was home she was barely present.

One day a babysitter found heavy bruises on Simon's tiny legs and reported it to the Department of Children and Family Services. Within hours Simon and his sister were whisked away into state custody. For the next couple of years they bounced around from foster home to foster home. Whenever they finally started to make an emotional connection to a family, they were moved to a new home. Eventually one of the families adopted the two children.

Simon grew into an angry teenager. In junior high he started experimenting with marijuana and alcohol. This together with his outbursts of pent-up rage caused him to get into trouble at school and eventually with the law. When Simon was in his late teenage years, he learned that his biological mother had died of a drug overdose. His father, however, had remarried and was living on the West Coast with his new family. Simon reserved a smoldering hatred for his biological father.

When you've been hurt, betrayed, or devastated by someone, sometimes people push you to get over it. "Move on. Forgive and forget." But forgiveness is not that easy. All reconciliation requires that someone pay a price. Scripture says, "Bear with each other and forgive one another if any of you has a grievance against someone. Forgive as the Lord forgave you."[1]

Our forgiveness is modeled on how Jesus forgave us. It is not merely pretending that nothing happened, but it is a willingness to absorb the pain and offense out of love for the other. Jesus, because of his deep love for us, absorbed all of our sin, hatred, anger, and rebellion and took it on himself on the cross. He literally paid the price for our sins. And this is what makes forgiveness difficult—having the resources and love in our hearts to willingly bear the pain and heartache others inflict on us, so we can be rightly related to them again.

Because there is no message more central to the biblical narrative than forgiveness, it is very important that we get this right. So much of the deadness we see in our own lives—so much of the hardness of heart—is rooted in the fact that we will not reciprocate what Christ has done for us. There are rumors floating around that forgiveness is worth the cost. The challenge of our lives is to risk that they are true. And often, it is a risk we are unwilling to take. This challenge brings us to Jonah. His story is about all of us really, but it's portrayed through a rebellious prophet who wrestled with the mercy of God.

GOD, DON'T HAVE MERCY

God speaks to Jonah with a simple command, "Go to Nineveh."

Jonah says, "No thanks," and instead goes to Tarshish, which is in the opposite direction. On the boat ride out of town, a storm forms and ultimately Jonah gets thrown into the sea and swallowed by a huge fish. Three days later he is vomited out onto dry land.

Again, God tells him to go to Nineveh. This time Jonah obeys, but reluctantly. Jonah gives an unconvincing, halfhearted prophecy to the citizens of Nineveh: "Forty more days and Nineveh will be overthrown."² That's it—just eight words with no threat of the display of God's righteous anger.

Throughout the Old Testament, prophets articulated warnings of impending judgment if they did not repent. They were great oracles who compelled the people to repentance. Not Jonah. He squeaks, "Forty more days and Nineveh will be overthrown." He doesn't even say who will overthrow Nineveh or what the people must repent from.

No one was more surprised than Jonah when the king of Nineveh repented. He issued an official decree and called on everyone to fast from food and water for the way that they had been living.

There are only four chapters in the book of Jonah, and the big twist comes in Chapter four: "But Jonah was greatly displeased and became angry."³ What a baffling response from the prophet. He gave a halfhearted prophecy with a few words and brought the city to its knees. The entire population of Nineveh listened, agreed, and repented. Compared to the success rates of some of the other biblical prophets, Jonah should have been delighted. So why was he upset?

It has to do with forgiveness.

Jonah prayed to the Lord:

O LORD, is this not what I said when I was still at home? That is why I was so quick to flee to Tarshish. I knew that you are a gracious and compassionate God, slow to anger and abounding in love, a God who relents from sending calamity. Now, O LORD, take away my life, for it is better for me to die than to live.[4]

Jonah seems to have gone off the deep end. He accused God of being gracious and compassionate, slow to anger and abounding in love. And Jonah was suicidal because of it. Do you resonate with Jonah's response? Maybe you would if you understood the world Jonah lived in.

A SPECIAL KIND OF BRUTALITY

Nineveh was the capital of Assyria, one of the great empires in the history of the world. The reign of the Assyrian Empire was unmatched. The Assyrians were also unmatched in their cruelty.

The Assyrians ruled by fear, oppression, intimidation, and terror. Historian Dan Carlin says the Assyrians invented terrorism.[*] Other empires that followed copied their barbaric practices. The kings of Assyria were known for boasting about their cruelty. For example, when a city staged a revolt against the Assyrian king Ashumasirpal, he declared:

> I built a pillar over the city gate and filleted all the chiefs who revolted and I covered the pillar with their skin. Some I impaled on the pillar on stakes. Some I bound to stakes around the pillar and I cut the limbs off the royal officers who had rebelled. Many captives among them, I burned with fire. I took some living captives and I cut off their

---

* Thanks to Shane Hipps for sharing some of his sources, research, and insights with me (Darren), including the work of Dan Carlin.

noses, their ears, and their fingers. Of many, I put out their eyes. These are the ones living.[5]

This is a word-for-word translation of his historical account of the incident.

When a city tried to revolt, the Assyrians would make an example out of them to the rest of the empire. Some historians say that the damage they inflicted was comparable to that of a nuclear bomb. There was one small exception. They would do it by hand. If a city tried to revolt, it was decimated. They would kill the livestock, torture and murder the children, set buildings on fire, tear up crops, and then plant thistles and weeds in the fields. Then they would spread salt throughout the soil so nothing could grow. In some cases they would divert an entire river through the city to destroy everything—to leave no structures at all, no living creatures, no trace that a community had ever prospered there.

At the end of the day, the Assyrians would get together to celebrate. They'd laugh, drink, and boast of their exploits. Their message was clear: if you try to resist, if you dare to revolt, you will pay. This was the legacy of the Assyrians.

But the Assyrians reserved a special kind of brutality for the Jews; one that was subtle, but more painful. Because the Jews had such a strong sense of ethnic heritage and identity, the Assyrians decided not to obliterate the race, but to dilute it. They invaded the northern kingdom of Israel and forced the Jews to marry the Assyrians. When the Jewish women gave birth, they produced a mixed race: half Jew, half Assyrian.

This generation was disowned and despised by both groups, particularly the Jews. The Jews believed that a faithful Jew would never marry an Assyrian. In fact, faithful Jews would die before they allowed that to happen. This half-breed people group became known as the Samaritans.

The Samaritans make several appearances in the New Testament. As a group they were hated, oppressed, and marginalized. The good Samaritan was obviously a part of this group. In the story of the ten lepers, the one who came back to say thank you to Jesus was a Samaritan. The woman at the well was also a Samaritan. Knowing the history of this people group sheds light on why they were so despised by the Jews.

Nineveh was one of the major cities in the Assyrian Empire, so you can see why Jonah hated it. God forgiving Nineveh was unthinkable to Jonah. Even the thought made him furious. He didn't want Nineveh to repent. He didn't want them to be forgiven. He wanted them to get what they deserved for their wickedness and cruelty. He would rather die than see these people receive God's mercy and grace. Even more, rather than Jonah being seen as a success by his people, he would be seen as a traitor, the one who let their enemies off for their sins.

Some historians call the Assyrians the "biblical-era Nazis." When my wife and I (Darren) visited Nuremberg, Germany, we stood where Hitler held his Nazi conventions, also known as the Nuremberg rallies. Imagine if Hitler, after annihilating six million Jews, came to God and said, "God, upon some deep reflection I have remorse about wiping out the Jewish people. To show you my sincerity, I'm going to fast from my food, and I'm going to have the SS, the Gestapo, and the guards from the concentration camps fast from food as well. I'm going to put on sackcloth. I'm sincerely sorry for what I've done. Will you forgive me?"

Imagine that God looked at Hitler and said, "Let me think about this. You murdered six million Jews. You are fasting from your food as a sign of contrition, putting on sackcloth. Yes, I think we're good now. You're free to go. No punishment. No judgment."

Just as Jonah was infuriated at the notion of the Ninevites (the Assyrians) receiving mercy, the thought of Hitler receiving the same forgiveness is unthinkable to us. Vengeance should be his lot, not forgiveness. It would seem more just for the world to operate under the premise of the Eastern principle of karma. If someone does something good, then the outcome should be positive. If someone does something bad or evil, then they should be punished. That is the equilibrium of the universe that makes sense to us.

REVENGE IS OUR RIGHT

Have you ever thought about how many movies are built around the central premise of revenge? *Kill Bill, Edge of Darkness, Man on Fire, V for Vendetta*, and the list goes on. We find ourselves cheering for the protagonist to seek out the perpetrators and give them what they deserve—retribution, wrath, vengeance. The problem with revenge is that although it brings retaliation, it rarely brings freedom. As Albert Schweitzer said, "Revenge . . . is like a rolling stone, which, when a man hath forced up a hill, will return upon him with a greater violence, and break those bones whose sinews gave it motion."[6]

Martin Luther King Jr. is famous for these words: "Darkness cannot drive out darkness; only light can do that. Hate cannot drive out hate; only love can do that."[7]

Revenge feels like it will quench the thirst of the pain. But it rarely does. Freedom is only found another way—the way of forgiveness.

God says:

> *Seek the* LORD *while he may be found;*
>> *call on him while he is near.*
> *Let the wicked forsake his ways*
>> *and the unrighteous their thoughts.*
> *Let them turn to the* LORD, *and he will have mercy*
>> *on them, and to our God, for he will freely pardon.*
> *"For my thoughts are not your thoughts,*
>> *neither are your ways my ways," declares the* LORD.
> *"As the heavens are higher than the earth,*
>> *so are my ways higher than your ways*
>> *and my thoughts than your thoughts."*[8]

It seems fair that people should be repaid for the evil they have done, but God says forgiveness is an even more potent force.

When Jesus died on the cross, he absorbed the sin of the world. It was painful, but he took it on. In forgiving, you may wrestle with a sense of injustice—the sense of rewarding actions that are hurtful, the sense that the people who have wronged you are getting away with something. But forgiveness is not a feeling; it's an action. It's not an emotion (though emotion is involved); it's a choice. Not an easy choice, but a choice. It's actually embedded in the word itself: *for-give*. You're giving a gift—a gift of forgiveness. It's a choice that you have to make, an action that you have to take. This is not something we can conjure up out of the will-power of sheer human kindness. It is only possible when God imparts his grace to us, the same grace that caused Jesus to suffer for our evil and sin.

The sweet part of forgiveness lies in the freedom you

experience once you've made the choice and taken action. It's hard to imagine what lies on the other side of forgiveness. Usually before you've forgiven someone it's difficult to see how freedom can emerge, how it could possibly be better than letting them get what they've got coming to them. It's a matter of perspective. Often we remain so focused on the one who perpetrated the evil deed that we don't see our own bondage to resentment or even hatred. But when you forgive, you're the one who is set free.

Forgiveness is one of the foremost themes in the New Testament. Jesus says to love your enemy and bless those who persecute you. The key messages in the stories of the good Samaritan, the prodigal son, and the woman at the well are about showing love to people who don't deserve it. It's the way Jesus showed love to tax collectors and prostitutes and ultimately to us by hanging on a cross.

RETALIATION OF LOVE

On Monday morning, October 2, 2006, Charles Roberts entered a one-room Amish school in Nickel Mines, Pennsylvania, armed with a gun. This thirty-two-year-old man opened fire on twenty-five horrified children. He killed five little girls, leaving others critically wounded. Then he turned the gun on himself and took his own life. This story captured the attention of the media not only in the United States, but also around the world. By Tuesday morning, fifty television crews had assembled in the small village of Nickel Mines. They stayed for five full days until the killer and the slain little girls were buried.

After leaving the funerals of their own children, the Amish community attended the funeral of the killer. The parents of the slain Amish girls greeted the killer's widow and his three children. If that wasn't extraordinary enough, the grieving parents helped establish a fund to support the killer's family. They did this because of what Christ had done for them. Within a week of the murders, the story of the Amish community's response was more prevalent than the incident itself. The term "Amish forgiveness" was the central theme in more than twenty-four hundred reports around the world. *The Washington Post*, *The New York Times*, *USA Today*, *Larry King*, *Oprah*, and dozens of other media outlets were astounded by the outrageous forgiveness of these Amish people.

"My ways are higher than your ways and my thoughts higher than your thoughts."

God wants us to receive forgiveness and extend forgiveness, and then to experience freedom—the best kind of life. The alternative is a miserable one. Jonah said, "Now, O LORD, take away my life, for it is better for me to die than to live."[9]

God knows that when we don't forgive, when we're bitter, when we harbor anger, we lose our lives—something inside of us starts to decay and die. Bitterness actually hurts us, and we don't experience freedom.

This is all very easy to say, isn't it? Maybe you have a specific situation in mind as you are reading this. This vision is compelling and full of hope, but actually living it out is often gut-wrenchingly difficult and complex. There are many misnomers circulating about forgiveness, especially among Christians. Here are six myths that we have come across many times:

Myth #1. Forgiving is the same as forgetting.

To forgive does not mean to forget. Most people will never forget the immense hurt done to them or to a loved one. But while you may never forget (and do not need to), the hope is to not dwell on or allow yourself to be defined by the hurt someone else has caused you.

Myth #2. Forgiving is the same as reconciling.

Reconciliation is not always possible or even best, particularly when you are in an ongoing abusive relationship. For other situations, you may desire reconciliation and that may be the ideal outcome, but it is not necessarily a prerequisite for forgiveness.

Myth #3. Forgiving is the same as excusing.

Forgiveness is not excusing the hurtful behavior. In fact, you usually need to process and recognize the intensity and extent of your pain and hurt to extend genuine forgiveness.

Myth #4. Forgiving will make you weak.

Extending forgiveness is not a sign of weakness; it's a sign of strength, courage, and resilient character. Offering forgiveness will liberate your heart, release your mind, and actually make you stronger.

Myth #5. Forgiving is a simple act or decision.

Forgiveness is often not a one-time choice; it takes time. It's a process. If someone close to you has betrayed or hurt you, it may take a significant amount of time to arrive at an authentic place of forgiveness.

Myth #6. Forgiving depends on the perpetrator admitting wrong.

Many feel they cannot extend forgiveness until there has been some ownership or admittance of wrongdoing. This is not the case. Sometimes that will never come. You can only control your own behavior.

Let's go back to the beginning of this chapter, to Simon. When he reached his early twenties, Simon had a life-changing encounter with Jesus. As his relationship with God deepened, he sensed that God was challenging him to forgive his dad. He wrestled with that idea. He thought, *My dad was not there for me. Why should he be able to get away with treating his own son like he did?*

But the more Simon got to know Jesus, the more he discovered the grace and compassion of God—the God who is slow to anger and abounding in love. It wasn't easy, but Simon started to release his anger. And one day he realized that he had forgiven his dad.

So, after more than fifteen years of not seeing him, he decided he was going to take a trip to visit his dad. He called him, said he wanted to meet, and asked him to come pick him up at the airport. His father agreed.

Because of his relationship with Jesus and his understanding of what God had done for him in Christ, Simon was transformed from an angry kid into a young man with a heart full of love. Instead of hating and resenting the man who deserted him, he wanted to hug him. On the plane Simon saw someone he knew and told him he was about to see his dad for the first time in over fifteen years. He told the whole story of how until recently he'd hated his dad, but that God helped him forgive him—his hate was replaced with love for him. He asked his friend if he would take a picture of the moment he hugged his dad.

When Simon shared this story with me, he showed me the picture of him hugging his dad. As I looked at this picture and reflected on the hatred and anger that had lasted for years, I thought to myself, *this may be the most powerful force in the world.*

When we forgive, we become like our heavenly Father. To forgive is to act like God. The greater the wound, the greater the forgiveness, and the greater the reflection of the heart of God.

God wants us to be released. He wants us to experience life— he wants to take out the heart of stone and give us a heart of flesh. There's a rumor that freedom really is possible. If you can get to the point of letting go of anger, resentment, and bitterness—there is new life, fresh hope, and immense freedom. God wants us to know that there is a better way to live. The rumors of freedom and forgiveness are true.

CHAPTER SEVEN

THE RADICAL INDIVIDUAL

Rumors of Commitment

Surely you know that if a man can't be cured of churchgoing, the next best thing is to send him all over the neighborhood looking for the church that "suits" him until he becomes a taster or connoisseur of churches . . . the search for a "suitable" church makes the man a critic where the Enemy* wants him to be a pupil.

—the demon Screwtape to Wormwood in
The Screwtape Letters* by C. S. Lewis

The Bible knows nothing of solitary religion.

—John Wesley

The eye cannot say to the hand, "I have no need of you."

—St. Paul to the Corinthians

---

* To those not familiar with *The Screwtape Letters*, "Enemy" here means God.

Someone recently came up to me (Jon) after one of our worship gatherings to give me some feedback. "I didn't mind the teaching," he said, "but I didn't like the worship."

I asked what he meant.

"I didn't get anything out of it," was his reply.

"Well," I said, "you must be confused."

He asked what I meant by that.

"The worship wasn't for you," I replied. "It was for God. Did you ask God what he thought about it?" He thought I was kidding, but I wasn't. "As far as I can tell biblically, it doesn't matter what you get out of worship, it's not for you. It's supposed to be something you offer, not something you receive."

I lovingly suggested he spend some time in the book of Revelation, chapters four and five, to discover who was supposed to "get something" out of worship.

He lovingly responded by never coming back to our church.

Conversations like this perplex me. How is it that we have reduced the life God offers to an economic exchange where autonomous individuals come to get their needs met? Why didn't this young man ask about the life of our church, about things that would tell him who we are, and what we were about as a people? How do you love one another? How do you care for the poor? How do you meet each other's practical needs? How do you teach your people to walk humbly with God?

His comments reveal a mind-set that has crept into our hearts. Many of us fall into these same patterns of thinking when we approach Christian community and our relationship with God. How did we get to the place where church is something primarily for "me" and a place I go to "get" something from it?

Have you ever wondered what it is that has shaped us into people who see things this way?

Many of us have a sense that this is not what God intended. We intuitively feel there are powerful yet subtle forces working to push us in individualistic directions. Some blame postmodern culture, others blame liberal theology, many of us blame consumerism; but I wonder if there is something even deeper than this. I wonder if the root of this aggressive individualism goes further back.

While searching for answers to these questions, I met an Australian cultural observer and pastor named Mark Sayers who has studied the roots of individualism. His analyses show a sharp contrast between the life God offers and the story told in our modern context.[1] Much of what follows is informed by his studies of the cultural development of the story of the radical individual.

THE STORY WE'VE BEEN SOLD

I (Jon) was playing in the park with my son, when he started acting out various lines by characters in cartoon films. I was having fun when I asked, "Why don't we invent our own characters and make up our own lines to say?"

He looked at me incredulously, and replied, "Why would we do that? The movies already tell us who we should be."

This is the heartbreaking reality that we want to focus on in this chapter. Illustrator Brad Holland wrote, "In Modernism, reality used to validate media. In Postmodernism, the media validate reality. If you don't believe this, just think how many times you've described some real event as being 'just like a movie.'"[2]

It's this idea that our culture tells us who to be that I want to explore and challenge, and I want to see if Jesus offers some insight into why our culture's story is killing us, and how his story leads us to a more full and abundant life.

But first, in order to discern our current situation, we need to understand the prolific changes that have taken place during the last seventy years. We are now at least three generations deep into our current framework. This means that if you ask your parents or grandparents for answers, they will tell you the same things, because they have been raised in the same story you have. As a culture we have simply forgotten any other way to live. So let's take a look at the roots of individualism and see why it's imperative we break free from its spell and take hold of the life God offers in the beauty of Christian community.

THE RADICAL YOU

After World War II, people grew increasingly disillusioned. They were looking for an explanation for the atrocities associated with the war. Hitler's regime caused many to doubt stories (metanarratives) that were thrust onto society. These seeds of suspicion were sown into the soil of American life.

This collective disillusionment embedded itself into the individual lives of the returning soldiers. No longer primarily interested in a national vision for life, the soldiers and their families pursued their own visions, their own individual dreams. This gave birth to places like Levitt Town, the first suburbs, and enabled the GIs to functionally privatize their lives. With the invention of the refrigerator, people could isolate themselves for days, stocked with food and entertainment. They had their own land, their own cars, and their own homes. And so the consumer version of the American dream was born. People began to pursue these things more and more rather than interacting with one another.

The first generation born into these years of unprecedented affluence and autonomy had a brewing sense of angst. They had no great war to fight in, no great evil to oppose, and they saw little in their world to give their passion and energy to. A young writer tapped into this angst with a novel that redefined what was to become the new youth culture. *On The Road*, written by Jack Kerouac, called a generation away from the predictability of their parents' lives into a life of constant experience and a rucksack revolution. Kerouac urged young people to go into the world without agenda, timetable, or responsibility. His call was away from the predictability of comfortable America into the wilds of the unknown. The seeds of rebellion and individualism were now bearing cultural fruit as a new kind of person began to come of age.

Hollywood executives began to pick up on this growing movement, so they created a new kind of hero whose impact we still feel today: James Dean. The *Rebel Without a Cause* motif resonated with the hearts of many young Americans. As the name suggests, the significance of this film is that Dean's character had nothing in his comfortable life to legitimately rebel against. He simply had a growing unease with the comfortable mediocrity of his parents' lives. Young men resonated with this story. And so began the popular incarnation of the radical individual.

The radical individual became the defining figure in popular media. Think about the cultural icons that followed actors like James Dean—Marlon Brando, John Wayne, Clint Eastwood, and James Bond. All represent the quintessential lone cowboy who rides into town with no relationships, no history, no connections, and takes on the world "his way." He womanizes and then goes back to his hardened self, no strings attached—no commitments.

Women experienced a shift in cultural identity as well. At first Hollywood portrayed women as chaste, refined, and modest. They were self-assured and dedicated to commitment. But Marilyn Monroe shattered that stereotype in her breakout film *Gentleman Prefer Blondes*. She became the first popular sex symbol, and her "dumb blonde" persona conquered the modern imagination.

But, arguably, the most definitive shift in the way women saw themselves was to come from Audrey Hepburn's cult classic *Breakfast at Tiffany's*. This film tells the story of Holly Golightly, a small-town girl from the South who comes to the big city to reinvent herself. Holly is "classy" but suffers from deep insecurity. Her response to her anxiety attacks, which she deems "getting the mean reds," is to go window-shopping at Tiffany's. When she is at Tiffany's, she feels like nothing in the world can go wrong.

This film popularized glamour for women—the ability to paste a confident, glamorous veneer over deep insecurity. The film continues to influence the fashion world as Hepburn's body shape became a benchmark in the industry. What is not widely known is that Hepburn's figure was not the result of diligence or genetics but rather the result of wartime deprivation. Hepburn grew up under Nazi occupation in the German-occupied Netherlands. The steep food regulations affected Hepburn's ability to put on weight her entire life. In essence, the popular vision of beauty in our world is more defined by Nazi brutality than by the way God intended the typical woman to look.

If *Breakfast at Tiffany's* put glamour on the map, then Brigitte Bardot pushed sexuality into the mainstream. She was the first movie star to establish sexuality as a woman's supreme asset.

Women began to consider where their sexuality put them in the competitive female hierarchy, rather than just considering how they appealed to men. Fast forward to the present day. The characters from the hit HBO series *Sex and the City* not only asserted their femininity, they also treated men the way men had been portrayed as treating women—as toys.

Under the guise of liberating women, Hollywood captured the minds of the women of the world to believe that being independent is superior to commitment, and that relationships exist only to meet personal needs.

From cultural icons of the past to today's rock, television, and movie stars, our lives have been remolded into the image of the world—the image of the radical individual.

FREEDOM WORSHIP?

The original *Matrix* film was a sensation. It asked brilliant questions about reality, hyperreality, and control. Pastors and commentators applauded the film, using it as a talking point for gospel conversations. But the second film in the series failed to deliver.

In *Matrix Reloaded*, we see the humans continuing to fight the machines in an effort to defend Zion, the last free city of humans. But what is Zion? What are the humans going to war for?

In one of the clearest, most illuminating (and disappointing) scenes of the film, Morpheus stands before the people of Zion and gives a *Braveheart*-esque speech that concludes with a celebration of the city's humanity. The "celebration," however, is a massive sexual rave-type party where autonomous individuals dance and grope with whomever they want. There's no sign of covenant or commitment. The lie perpetuated by this scene is that ultimate freedom, the kind worth dying for, equates to autonomous sexuality without commitment.

The biblical imagery in the film got me thinking about what our culture presents as salvation. Salvation for the radical individual could be summed up as complete autonomy, self-definition, and minimal commitment with maximum personal pleasure.

But is this kind of salvation, this kind of life, really Zion? Is this the kingdom of heaven on earth that Jesus has come to establish? Is Jesus' vision that we live as disconnected individuals who use everything, including him, to meet our personal needs? Are we going to drift through our lives without ever committing to others, from church to church, friendship to friendship, marriage to marriage, without encountering the life God offers?

Perhaps the reason God seems more like a rumor than a reality to so many of us is that we expect him to confirm something that simply isn't true. He doesn't want us to live as consumeristic individuals who are afraid of commitment and thrive on selfishness. He offers something profoundly better.

STILL GETTING NOTHING OUT OF GOD

In my mind I often revisit the conversation with the young man who got "nothing out of worship." I find myself asking what it would take to liberate him from the spell of radical individualism. How do we take people who are discipled by our culture and transform them into a community of selfless generosity? And how do we do that for ourselves?

These claims, that "life is better without authority, covenant, commitment, or accountability" sounded hauntingly familiar. They are the same empty claims that Satan temped Eve with in the garden of Eden.

Before the fall, we lived in perfect union with God, each other, the world, and ourselves. Everything was in its rightful place. There was a beautiful connection between God, Adam, and Eve. Satan, who had chosen the path of radical independence, knew that there was nothing but death apart from God and he wanted to strike back at God's heart, so he tempted Eve with a false promise that eventually caused her to stumble and eat from the Tree of Knowledge. Disobedience did give her understanding, but it didn't give her life. She was cast out of God's presence, and we still feel that isolation today as a deep angst in our souls.

The modern promises of our world are just repackaged versions of the original lie. The last seventy years have been particularly effective in getting us to believe that we are not accountable to anyone—and better off that way. But the truth continues to haunt us that though we are the most free, most independent people in history, we are also the most isolated, most lonely, and most fractured. We have knowledge but, like Eve, we are learning that it comes at an incredible price: separation from God and isolation from one another.

REDISCOVERING LIFE WITH GOD AND HIS PEOPLE

I had another person come up to me after one of our worship gatherings. From the outside this man looked incredibly successful. In his early thirties, stylish, with an air of confidence and power, he seemed deeply moved by his encounter with truth that morning. He wanted to connect with me so he could process some of the things that had taken place in his heart. We set up a time to meet, and at coffee he shared a deeply moving story.

Rick came to the city in his late teenage years with a vision to make a name for himself. He started out as an intern at a PR firm but quickly realized he had a knack for promotions. So he launched his own company in his early twenties, promoting anyone and anything that could build his firm. He began to make his way into the inner networks of Manhattan power and ended up being recruited by one of the top PR firms in the city. Meanwhile, he had more money than he knew what to do with, more casual sex than he ever thought possible, celebrity access that made others envious, and the kind of success that was the hallmark of the Big Apple.

I asked him what brought him to church. He replied that one of the receptionists at his firm was a devout Christian, and frustratingly so. She was the "naïve kind" that didn't even get drunk at the office Christmas party. One day Rick asked what she was doing over the weekend, and she shared she was going on a church retreat. Rick dismissed it as a weekend of purgatory, but when he asked the receptionist about her community, she glowed.

She talked about their acceptance of one another, how they loved each other despite their pasts and mistakes, and how they were learning not to find their identity in their performance. She talked about how her friends had recently raised money to buy a beautiful wig for a friend's mother who had lost her hair during chemotherapy treatments. She explained how they were committed to living "in the way of Jesus," and she casually invited him to our church.

During the next few weeks, he began to look below the surface of his life and realized there was a profound sense of isolation in his soul. He was alienated from his family, had to keep up an image in front of his associates, enjoyed no lasting substantive relationships, and was alone. With deep cynicism, he made his way to church. Embarrassed to be seen there, he walked in late, sat in the balcony, and left before the service ended. Although it was a foreign environment, something kept him coming back—the contrarian idea that there was a starving part of his soul that could only be nourished through commitment to something larger than himself. Over coffee, he asked me if I could shed some light onto how Jesus and the church fit into his strange longings.

Losing Life in Order to Find It

I started by telling Rick that the longing he was feeling was actually for reconciliation with Jesus. Jesus calls us out of our own attempts to manage life and struggle through our existence. He doesn't invite us into some sort of general religious spirituality, but into union with him, the source of all life. He calls us out of our normal human experience, into finding the richness and fullness of life in union with him.

"Whoever wants to save their life will lose it, but whoever loses their life for Me will find it," Jesus said. "If anyone comes to Me, and does not hate his own father and mother and wife and children and brothers and sisters, yes, and even his own life, he cannot be My disciple."[3]

I went on to explain to Rick that Jesus is calling us to hate our own natural lives because they are marred with sin, guilt, shame, and death. He wants us to turn away from the things that are killing our hearts and separating us from God. He calls us to a life of discipleship, covenant, and commitment that ultimately leads to eternal life. He is so passionate about the full restoration of our hearts that he will not accept mediocre substitutes. I shared that Jesus is the vine and that life comes from union with his love. Though surprised, Rick seemed open. So I continued.

Paul defined this new spiritual reality in Ephesians 2. He used metaphors that progress in their intensity. The first thing he said was that we become citizens of the kingdom of God. Our allegiance shifts to God above all else. The next metaphor he used was that of a family—we become members of the household of God. This means that our relational loyalty shifts to other Christians. We cannot live independently of other believers and only think of our own needs. We become a part of the body, the family.

The next, and most intense, metaphor is that of a temple. Paul wrote that we are bricks God uses to build a holy temple where he will dwell. Paul made the incredible claim that no individual brick is big enough to contain the presence of God. It's all of us coming together, cementing our lives in love and covenant faithfulness that creates a community big enough for God to be truly present in.

After my coffee with Rick, we continued to connect and I watched our church do a beautiful job of enfolding him into the life of our community. Though not without real challenges, Rick committed his life to Christ and connected to a group of believers who gather weekly to share their stories and struggles and to spur one another on in the journey. He serves regularly with projects to raise money for wells in Africa and is committed to serving others in the church.

Jesus' way of commitment is in stark contrast to the radical individualism of our age. We find God's life unleashed in our own through the presence of others, not through autonomy. When the pivotal moments of our lives come, God's vision is that the body of Christ will surround us with the life and love of God in real and tangible ways.

———
———

When they stopped by the home of seventy-year-old Vincenzo Ricardo in the Hampton Bays, police found his mummified body still sitting in front of his television, which was surprisingly still turned on. It was surprising because Ricardo had been dead for more than a year and no one noticed. The police had only come to his home because someone reported a burst pipe, which was leaking water down the side of his home. A month before the shocking discovery, neighbors at a party questioned why they had not seen him in a while. "We never thought to check on him," said neighbor Diane Devon.

Police officials believe that he died in December 2005 and they found it strange that his electricity was still on all this time. Even stranger is that his mailbox was overflowing and yet no one seemed to notice, even though passersby could clearly see it.[4]

Everyone seemed to only have thought about him for a moment and just assumed he was probably fine, when a simple visit might have alerted them to a problem. What a tragic indictment of our time. The decaying body of a lonely man still perched in front of a medium that propagates the ideal that you're better off alone. But God's vision is different.

Not long ago I (Darren) received an e-mail from Joan, a woman in our church. She told me her teenage son, Will, had recently been diagnosed with leukemia. She said there were a couple of families from our church who were going to go to their house to pray for ten minutes. Our family decided to join them. When we pulled our car into the subdivision we noticed we couldn't get anywhere near their house. In fact there were cars lining the streets and we had a long walk to get to their home.

Joan recorded her thoughts in her blog that evening:

No one could have prepared me for these sweet ten minutes tonight. You see, God showed up in person at our door
tonight and in our yard and on our front porch and on the
swings and on the playsets and next to the trees in front.
God is fully present here all the time like he is at your house,
but tonight he physically encircled our house. How often do
you get to see that? I remember sitting in Will's room looking out the window as people walked up, and they just kept
coming and coming. I remember sobbing as I looked out to
the backyard. Around 200 orange ribbons were made for
leukemia, and not one of them was left. And there were bal-
loons with the words "I am there in their midst." I was told
there were cars all the way down the street.

My wife and daughters and I held hands with more than two
hundred people from our church, and we circled their home and
prayed for Will. Young people, older people, people of different
ethnicities and vocations all gathered together as the church. We
stood with this family and went before God with them and for
them. Rather than allowing a family to suffer in isolation, two
hundred people formed a human circle that became a portal of the
arms of Jesus. It's true. God showed up.[5]

Jesus prayed that his disciples would be one just as he and his
Father are one. Then the world would know that he was sent from
the Father. There's nothing more beautiful than covenant love.

We have an unbelievable opportunity to model to the world
that covenant is a better way. May these rumors of commitment
become a defining reality in our day.

CHAPTER EIGHT

LOVING BENEATH THE SURFACE

Rumors of Community

The English word hospitality originates from the same Latin root as the word hospital. A hospital is literally a "home for strangers." Of course, it has come to mean a place of healing. There is a link between being welcomed and being healed.

—Skye Jethani

Above all, love each other deeply, because love covers over a multitude of sins.

—Peter

I (Jon) have had the same meeting hundreds of times in my life. Someone wants to grab a cup of coffee and talk. I almost always know what it is going to be about. At some point in this hour-long conversation I will hear the words "I have been hurt by the church." Let's face it, no matter how compelling the vision of community, people are still hesitant to really engage. Because of the breakdown of relationships and the pain associated with broken promises, community can sound like a punishment rather than a reward. Many of us are lonely yet paralyzed by the fear of exposing our hearts to others. Neil Gaiman put it like this:

> Have you ever been in love? Horrible isn't it? It makes you so vulnerable. It opens your chest and it opens up your heart and it means that someone can get inside you and mess you up . . . . Love takes hostages. It gets inside you. It eats you out and leaves you crying in the darkness, so simple a phrase like "maybe we should be just friends" turns into a glass splinter working its way into your heart. It hurts. Not just in the imagination. Not just in the mind. It's a soul-hurt, a real gets-inside-you-and-rips-you-apart pain. I hate love.[1]

ENEMIES OF LOVE

One of the great challenges we face in moving into community is the incurable need for the approval of others. It's so hard to keep putting our hearts out there and risk rejection from the rest of the group. This leaves us unsure of our social standing, scrambling to fit in wherever we can. British author Alain de Botton described this angst as "status anxiety." He articulated it this way:

> The attention of others matters to us because we are afflicted by a congenital uncertainty as to our own value, as

a result of which affliction we tend to allow others' appraisals to play a determining role in how we see ourselves. Our sense of identity is held captive by the judgments of those we live among . . . . Our "ego" or self-conception could be pictured as a leaking balloon, forever requiring the helium of external love to remain inflated, and ever vulnerable to the smallest pinpricks of neglect. There is something at once sobering and absurd in the extent to which we are lifted by the attentions of others and sunk by their disregard.[2]

Many of us have experienced this. I (Jon) once heard someone say that we get our sense of worth from the persons whose opinions we value the most. This process starts early in our lives. You can probably remember wanting to fit in with the cool kids in elementary school, or obsessing about your appearance to impress a certain group or someone you had a crush on. Rather than diminishing in adulthood, it only increases.

What is a résumé? It's nothing more than an attempt to make ourselves look good so that people will choose us over others. What is dating? Dressing and acting our very best in the hopes we will be accepted romantically. Seeing others as competition flows through our lives.

This trap leads us to define ourselves by our outward appearance and hinders us from exposing our real selves. "So from now on we regard no one from a worldly point of view," Paul wrote in his letter to the Corinthian church. "Though we once regarded Christ in this way, we do so no longer. Therefore, if anyone is in Christ, the new creation has come: The old has gone, the new is here!"[3]

We should not judge people by worldly standards, but as God

sees them: dearly loved children with whom he has great patience and for whom he has great affection. Our identity does not stem from our appearance, accomplishments, or accolades. We don't have to hand God our moral résumé or impress him with our performance. Because of Jesus, we are fully accepted in God's sight.

So what does biblical community look like? How is it different from worldly experiences of community based on image and performance?

KNOWN AND ACCEPTED, ACCOUNTABLE AND CHALLENGED

Consider how the social network profile has impacted our lives. Consider how most of us prepare it. We work hard to craft the best possible image of ourselves. We take our best photos—from the best angles—that show us living incredible lives. (Have you ever put up a photo that highlights your double chin?) We carefully fill out the educational information to show that we are intelligent and qualified. We rename our job titles to spin them into higher-level positions. We make sure to include indie music and film so that we appear to have a unique and artsy side, while accepting friend requests from people we've never met in the hopes of looking more popular.

The problem with this is that it can bleed into our real lives. We can become afraid to show weakness or pain or doubt or struggle, because we feel people will reject us as less than what we pretend to be. But if you wear a mask or hide behind a profile, you give people the chance to love only your mask or profile. How heartbreaking and lonely. You fail to give others the chance to love you for your true self.

Many of us feel trapped behind our worldly labels and crave being seen for who we really are. Don't you long for a community where you can be known, loved, and challenged? In the book *White Teeth*, author Zadie Smith tells a story about a Bangladeshi man employed as a waiter in an Indian restaurant in London. He works till 3:00 a.m., makes terrible tips, and hates it all. In an effort to be known, he wishes he could wear a giant sign around his neck with the following words written on it:

> I am not a waiter. I have been a student, a scientist, a soldier, my wife is called Alsana, we live in East London but we would like to move north. I am a Muslim but Allah has forsaken me or I have forsaken Allah, I'm not sure. I have a friend Archie—and others. I am forty-nine but women still turn in the street sometime.[4]

What do you want people to know about you? If you could wear a sign around your neck, what would it read? The beauty of our faith is that God sees past our labels and appearance, through to our true selves, to our hearts. He sees our hopes, fears, longings, dreams, insecurities, and doubts and accepts us and loves us anyway. Biblical community is this exact kind of intimacy and acceptance: learning to lower our masks and love one another for who we truly are.

Challenged

God's love extends beyond knowledge and acceptance into intimacy and challenge. This is the second part of biblical community that leads us to life. We live in a world of unprecedented independence. The opportunities to give in to temptation have increased while accountability has decreased. We can drift from church to church, from small group to small group, without people ever holding us accountable to living lives worthy of God.

Most of us have been conditioned to believe that religion is a private thing and that our relationship with God has no real implications for those around us. Nothing could be further from the truth. We *need* the truth spoken into our lives. It's hard to follow Jesus, and we need words of encouragement and vision. The world we live in is full of deception that continually hardens our hearts to the things of God.

That is why we need to be involved with other Christians who will keep us in check and challenge our decisions—people who will speak love and grace into us. When people accept us, as God has done in Christ, it creates an atmosphere of trust. So how do we move past the "social network profile" community into a place where we can be known, accepted, and challenged? We do this by understanding the pathway of love.

Loving Beneath the Surface of Our Lives

In the book *Why Am I Afraid to Tell You Who I Am?* John Powell suggests there's a journey all relationships must go through in order to become truly transparent and reach a place of love.[5]

The journey looks like this:

1. Cliché

2. Fact

3. Opinion

4. Emotion

5. Transparency

Let me give you an example of how I have experienced this. First, dreaded cliché rears its head. When people find out that I am from Australia, they immediately draw upon Australian clichés in an attempt to connect with me. They use horrible accents and say things like "G'day mate" and "Throw another shrimp on the barbie." They ask what it was like to grow up in the Outback, and whether or not we had pet kangaroos.[6] I quickly help them move to the second level of the relational journey: fact.

I grew up in a small suburb on the outskirts of a city of one million people. I have seen only a few kangaroos in my life and I have never ridden one to school. My parents were working-class people, and I spent my entire life in the suburbs. After I deconstruct the cliché with the facts, we are able to go a little deeper.

We then move to the realm of opinion to further draw out a person's heart. What do you think of religion? Politics? Sexuality? Economics? Movies? We are trying to see what categories people fit into so we can get a picture of their preferences and tastes. When this happens, we begin to humanize others and move below the surface.

Have you ever been in a situation where people were progressing through this pathway in a conversation, but then there was a difference of opinion and things heated up? Maybe the volume increased; maybe others in the conversation began to glance sideways at each other. We cringe at this point of tension and awkwardness and can feel threatened, criticized, or even attacked. This is interaction at the next level of intimacy: emotion. Emotions are hard and personal, affect us deeply, touch our souls directly, even control us.. What's our first instinct when we encounter emotions? Some try to settle things down. It's also common to retreat into shallower forms of community. We back down with phrases such as, "Well, that's okay; we just have different opinions."

But when we do this, we fail to love others past the point of our discomfort, and we never really learn to trust or disagree or share our true selves without fear of rejection or condemnation. We feel we can never be transparent. In relationships, these are defining moments; we either push through emotion to transparency, or retreat to opinions. And if we choose retreat, we normally go backward in the conversation journey. We talk about facts and make judgments about clichés.

But when we take the risk to listen and disagree and push through the discomfort of emotion, we come to a place of rare community where we can be our true selves. This kind of transparency is rare because we are used to retreating to shallow relationships. Strong emotions then, rather than being the thing that drives us apart, can actually be the tool that brings us together.

Isn't this what Jesus has done for us? Didn't he come to do away with all the religious clichés and tell us the truth about who God is? Didn't he come to set the record straight about God in the midst of our confusion? Didn't he come to reveal that God is for us and not against us—that he loves us and seeks to know us and has come that we might have life to the fullest?

Didn't Jesus come to give us God's opinion about things like faith, holiness, grace, truth, justice, righteousness, and love? Didn't Jesus tell us the hard truths about what God is passionate about? And didn't Jesus model vulnerability on our behalf—weeping at pain and brokenness, beaten and stripped naked and transparent for the entire world to see?

And didn't he risk death to do this in the hopes that we would respond in love and be honest about our true state of sin? Didn't he become vulnerable and transparent in an attempt to draw us into an authentic relationship with him?

———

A couple in our church was struggling in their marriage; the wife didn't know that her husband was having an affair. After a sermon on relationships, they were talked into attending a small group. The husband in particular was skeptical that a Christian marrieds group was going to do anything to help him. But they reluctantly agreed to go.

About halfway through the meeting, couples started to share. One husband told how he had cheated on his wife and then shared how the members of the group had stepped in to save him from himself. They lovingly confronted him and committed to walk through the whole situation with a vision of God's magnificent grace and restoration.

His wife then went on to share that though she was obviously devastated at first, she was able to find support, love, and acceptance from the small group. The love and commitment modeled by the group proved to be the impetus for the couple to make it through the brutal time and experience full marital restoration. The couple thanked the community for knowing them, accepting them, and loving them through the hardest season of their lives.

The skeptical man attending the group was absolutely

dumbfounded. How did this couple have the courage to expose all their dirty laundry to a group like this? And why didn't the people throw them out the door and tell them they were going to hell? He could not fathom that this sort of transparency existed.

Almost against his will, in front of this community of strangers, he blurted out, "I'm having an affair as well, and my wife doesn't know anything about it!" Silence followed, then his wife's anger, disbelief, and shock. But the majestic grace of God also followed, unleashed through the power of community.

This same community welcomed the distressed couple. The man broke off the affair; the group paid for their counseling and smothered them in practical kindness. The group rallied around them and during the most heartbreaking parts of restoration seemed to hold their lives as bandages against the wounds. The couple made it through—though the pain was great. Today they help lead the marriage ministry at our church.

This sort of community, the kind that lets you put it all out there without fear of guilt, shame, or condemnation is one of Christianity's great gifts to the world. First modeled by Jesus and rumored among his followers, it exists as one of the primary tools God uses to move from profiles to real people, to bring statues to life and transform hearts of stone into hearts of flesh.

A Vision for Suspended Space

It's one thing to have a longing for community; it's another to find the path that leads you there. But how do we go about culti-vating this kind of environment on a regular basis? How does this rare gift of being known and challenged become normal in our lives and the lives of the people around us?

I once heard a young Irish philosopher share a concept that clarifies the kind of sacred space we are talking about.[7] He called it "suspended space." Suspended space is an intentional, cultivated environment where everyone leaves their worldly identities at the door. For just an hour at a time, people pretend they're neither rich nor poor, male nor female, white nor black, married nor single—they simply accept their identity as children of God.

During this hour people are free to share whatever weighs on their hearts without fear of reprimand or judgment. They listen to one another. They care for one another. They are *present* with one another. This may not sound too radical, but where else in our culture does a space like this exist?

Think about the way many small groups work regarding vulnerability. Someone, let's call him Joe, drops an emotional bomb in the group, and immediately several people begin to lecture. One person cuts Joe off midconfession and suggests, "This is not an appropriate venue to share things like this." Another jumps in to correct Joe's bad behavior. Someone else interrupts to critique him on making unwise choices. And another chimes in with criticism of Joe's immaturity and character flaws, while another person begins to unfold a personal running commentary about how they have made similar mistakes. All Joe wanted was a safe place to find empathy—a sympathetic listening group who accepts him, no strings attached.

It is almost impossible to find this kind of space in the world today, but it is worth fighting for and worth cultivating. Paul said, "Accept one another, then, just as Christ accepted you, in order to bring praise to God."[8]

I (Jon) was at church recently when I encountered this suspended space in a powerful way. I like to greet people as they are coming in. On this particular night I was paying close attention to the kinds of people entering the church. I was blown away by what I saw.

The person greeting at the door was a member of our community who happened to be, until recently, homeless. He dressed in his best clothes on Sunday nights and served on our greeting team. Then a woman who is on the cast of a popular TV show walked in. He not only greeted her, but they hugged and called each other by name. It turns out they are a part of the same missional community.*

I went upstairs to the back of the room, where one of our leaders proceeded to introduce me to a friend he had brought. He whispered to me that his friend was not a Christian, and that it was his first time ever in a church.

As I walked to the front of the sanctuary, I bumped into a woman who had recently come to Christ. A former atheist, she wanted to tell me about what she was discovering about her new identity as a child of God. I was high-fived by one of the students in our youth group, a kid from the projects who had recently become a Christian, while a Wall Street broker prayed with a friend who was in crisis. We all sang a song, written by one of our worship leaders that contained the following lyrics: "We sing as one, Lord; we are your children; pour out your Spirit upon the broken."

As I looked around the room I was overwhelmed. I could not think of another room in the whole city where the recently homeless, famous, lost, newly found, rich, poor, and everything in between could raise their voices and sing as one. I imagined

---

* In our church we have neighborhood groups called missional communities whose purposes are to regularly serve and love our neighbors, care for one another, and promote justice in ways that clearly show the love and character of Jesus.

how pleasing this must be to God, to have a place of mercy and grace that was willing to suspend the normal social categories and embrace everybody into the family of God.

Homes As Hospitals

In *The Divine Commodity*, Skye Jethani says,

> Our homes are to be hospitals—refuges of healing radiating the light of heaven. And our dinner tables are to be operating tables—the place where broken souls are made whole again. In our churches people should find rest from their battle for acceptance and release from the lie that they are nothing more than the goods they possess. When we lower our defenses, when we remove our façades and our peepholes, and we begin to be truly present with one another—then the healing power of the gospel can begin its work.[9]

Jesus said we are to love one another as he loved us, and Paul said that we are to make room for each other's faults because of our love.[10] I can't help but wonder what would happen if Christians cultivated this relational transparency and strived to fill their lives with suspended space. What would happen if our homes became hospitals for our wounded neighbors, our lunch breaks became cathedrals for our searching coworkers, and our coffee shops became temples where people encounter Jesus in all of his beauty?

In a competitive, judgmental world like ours, I believe people would find out that the rumors are true—that we are, in fact, handiwork. We are coming to life, and it's happening as the kingdom of love comes crashing into our worlds.

CHAPTER NINE

THE GREENROOM

Rumors of Justice

Americans, Irish people, are good at charity. We like to give, and we give a lot, even those who can't afford it. But justice is a higher standard.

—Bono

"Sometimes I would like to ask God why he allows poverty, suffering, and injustice when he could do something about it." "Well, why don't you ask him?" "Because I am afraid he would ask me the same question."

—Anonymous

Speak up for those who cannot speak for themselves;
    ensure justice for those being crushed.

—Proverbs 31:8 NLT

Several years ago I (Darren) had coffee with a friend to catch up on life. She was a gifted singer-songwriter who had written several hits in Contemporary Christian Music. For the last five years, she had traveled throughout the United States and the world, singing, preaching, and inspiring people to evangelism. Over coffee she told me she was going to stop her traveling ministry and start serving a Christian humanitarian organization that worked predominantly in Africa.

In addition to this, she was going to sell her house and completely downsize her lifestyle. She told me she was captured by the idea of "living simply, so others can simply live." I listened intently and was really surprised by her passion and resolve to follow through with her new convictions.

"But what about preaching the gospel?" I asked her.

"Preach the gospel?" she said. "I'm trying to live the gospel."

I couldn't help but think she was walking away from the central biblical mandate. What she was doing was admirable and sacrificial, but a less imperative mission. She explained that this organization had highly developed initiatives on the ground in Africa. They were going to stimulate the local economy so that countries could begin to be self-sustaining. I enjoyed our conversation, but I was disappointed. I felt she was losing her way.

A short time later, I was in a small-group Bible study and we were unpacking the topic of justice. The man leading the group had studied the topic of biblical justice extensively and wanted to share some of his insights. I honestly thought I knew the biblical position on justice and was content to watch and let everyone else learn.

But as we began discussing the themes I learned some of the most illuminating insights I have heard as a Christian. Maybe my friend was onto something. Maybe it was me who was losing my way. Turns out, I knew very little about biblical justice.

DOUBLE MEANING

Throughout the Old Testament, the words "righteousness and justice" appear together. They are two inseparable themes, and they show up over and over and over again. In Psalms we read, "The LORD loves righteousness and justice; /the earth is full of his unfailing love."[1] Again in the Psalms we find: "Clouds and thick darkness surround him; /righteousness and justice are the foundation of his throne"[2] and "The Lord works for righteousness /and justice for all the oppressed."[3]

The prophet Amos wrote, "But let justice roll on like a river, /righteousness like a never-failing stream!"[4] Interestingly in the New Testament *justice* and *righteousness* do not show up together at all. I remember the gentleman leading the study asking us if any of us wondered about this.

Then he explained that in the New Testament the Greek word for *righteousness* is the word *dikaiosuné*, which is where we get the English word *righteousness*. But then he surprised me. "The Greek word *dikaiosuné* does not *only* mean righteousness," he said, "it also means justice."

What a revelation, and an important one. Most of us read the word *righteousness* and think nothing of justice. Could it be that we have thought of righteousness only in terms of the atonement, and neglected the idea that justice is central to God's heart? Could it be that we have missed the full meaning of this word for so long? I contacted a widely known and deeply respected New Testament scholar to see if this was theologically accurate. If this *was* true, then it would have radical implications for my understanding of the gospel. Sure enough, he confirmed this was true. *Dikaiosuné* means "righteousness and justice."

This new information changes things. Think of a few of the familiar passages you may know that contain the word *righteousness*. What if you read those verses adding *justice* to them? Let's try it:

> But seek first his kingdom and his righteousness *[and justice]*, and all these things will be given to you as well.[5]

> God made him who had no sin to be sin for us, so that in him we might become the righteousness *[and justice]* of God.[6]

> He himself bore our sins in his body on the tree, so that we may die to sins and live for righteousness *[and justice]*.[7]

It changes things, right? For me, I realized I had neglected an important part of the gospel for most of my life. I had subconsciously bought into the notion that evangelism—reconciling people with God—embodied the entire Christian message and that acts of justice were optional initiatives for Christians looking for extra credit from God. Justice is not a peripheral piece of our mission; it is a central mandate in following Jesus.

A BRAND APART

Think about the best-known brands in the world. When we see the Nike swoosh, we associate it with great athletic products. The swoosh looks like a checkmark, as if they have everything figured out. Based on their ad campaigns and their premier endorsements—Michael Jordan, LeBron James, Kobe Bryant—we believe that if we "Just Do It" we will, somehow, feel better about ourselves.

And what about the Apple computer logo? When we see it we are reminded that we are innovators, artists, and those who have drunk the Kool-Aid. What about the Starbucks sign? This temptress was famous in seventeenth-century mythology for seducing sailors onto rocks, so their ships would wreck and their treasure could be stolen. One could argue that, with four-dollar coffees, little has changed. These brands have the power to evoke an emotional response.

What about the most famous logo in the world? What do people think when they see the cross of Christ? Think about the makeup of this symbol. The cross contains two lines, one vertical and one horizontal. Embedded in the central symbol of Christianity we find the church's mission depicted by these lines. We find the vertical and horizontal work that Jesus accomplished on the cross—humanity reconciled vertically with God and horizontally with one another.

In Micah 6:8 we see a great example of this horizontal reconciliation: "to act justly and to love mercy" (NIV). The last part of this verse is the vertical reconciliation with God: "to walk humbly with your God"—live under his Lordship, with humility under God's rule and reign. This verse offers a complete view of gospel living, reconciliation with God and with each other.

In today's culture, justice is gaining popularity. Everyone's talking about justice. But what *is* justice? It can be a nuanced topic. There is retributive justice, as in the criminal justice system, is where a person receives the appropriate punishment or consequence for their crime. There is social justice, which primarily deals with the distribution of wealth and power.

And then there is biblical justice, which is more holistic. Biblical justice is built upon the *imago dei*: The premise that every human being is made in the image of God. We reflect our Creator.

Major Campbell Roberts of the Salvation Army described biblical justice like this:

> The justice of God requires that special concern be shown to the poor, the widows, the orphans, and for the immigrants (referred to in Scripture as the sojourners). In fact, the litmus test of Scripture on whether justice is being done is the plight of the poor and the needy in society. The true measure of justice is how the most vulnerable members of the community make out.[8]

We need to understand, however, the difference between compassion and justice. If we are not careful, we can begin to define them the same way when they are, in fact, very different. Compassion is often a step toward justice. We show compassion by bringing fresh water to a village because the water supply is contaminated.

Justice, on the other hand, entails investigating why the water is contaminated to begin with. Perhaps the investigation uncovers a factory upstream polluting the water. Justice seeks to stop the pollution at its source so that the people can have fresh water and thrive autonomously. Giving them clean water is compassion. Fixing the source of the pollution is justice.

As many of us have experienced, compassion and justice are inextricably linked. In the Psalms we read about God's heart for the oppressed: "Give justice to the poor and the orphan; /uphold the rights of the oppressed and the destitute. /Rescue the poor and helpless; /deliver them from the grasp of evil people."[9]

Gary Haugen, president of the International Justice Mission, said:

> Coming to understand God's compassion for the oppressed, and the way he suffers with them, has completely transformed my understanding of God. His real presence amid the horrendous injustice of our earth has finally allowed me to understand why God hates injustice so much. I have had to imagine what it would be like if I, like my God, had to watch, hear and witness every brutal act of injustice on the earth, every day . . . What must it be like for God to be present, this year, at the rape of all the world's child prostitutes, at the beatings of all the world's prisoners of conscience, at the moment the last breath of hope expires from the breast of each of the millions of small children languishing in bonded servitude . . . If we had to see and hear it every day like our God does, we would hate injustice, too.[10]

We would not only hate it the way God does, but it would shock us into action.

The poverty numbers in the world today are staggering. More than three billion people (almost half the world) live on $2.50 or less per day and struggle to obtain food and other necessities for survival.[11] The sick irony is that there is five times enough food to feed the entire world. There are thirty-three million people infected with HIV/AIDS, with twenty-five million in Sub-Saharan Africa alone.[12] And more than 1.1 billion people lack access to clean drinking water. Thirty-nine hundred children die every day because of dirty water or poor hygiene.[13]

Most of us read these outlandish numbers while sipping our four-dollar lattes. Often crises cause us to respond monetarily, but then we move on with our lives. Solving injustice isn't about throwing money at a problem. It's about fixing the root of the problem. As Christians, we have an obligation and responsibility to answer the clarion call of injustice not just with our cash, but also with our very lives.

What if the world, when it looks at the sign of the cross, saw not just a people of compassion, but also a people deeply committed to establishing worldwide biblical justice? Not just the action of giving care and filling the needs of the poor and destitute, but a people moved to solving the systemic problems behind the injustices of the world as well. What kind of beautiful message would this be for the world? Christians—a brand set apart.

GOD'S PLAN: YOU

In first-century Jewish culture, when a rabbi was praying, people would gather around and study his prayers in order to understand what his theology was. When Jesus was teaching his disciples, he said, "This, then, is how you should pray: . . . [May] your kingdom come, your will be done, on earth as it is in heaven."[14] Jesus' prayer was not that souls would be saved so that people could go to heaven. Jesus told us to pray that God's kingdom would come here, now.

In the Old Testament, God mandated that every fiftieth year would be a year of Jubilee. This was a year when debts were forgiven and land was returned to the original owners. So the rich and the poor were all leveled out. If a poor family had made bad financial decisions and lost their land, then the year of Jubilee would restore that land back to the family—giving them a fresh start. Every fifty years all the land was equaled out again, closing the chasm between the extremely poor and the extremely wealthy. In an agrarian society, where land represented revenue, this was revolutionary.

So much of the injustice in the world today is over land rights. In places like Africa and the Middle East, land rights and ownership drive massive international contention. Some of the most overt discriminatory issues of injustice in our world today involve racial discrimination, gender inequality, extreme poverty, education inequality, the AIDS pandemic, and unthinkable atrocities involving children, as well as adults, in sex trafficking.

Have you ever wondered why God doesn't do something about this? Gary Haugen responds to this question this way: "God has a plan to help bring justice into the world. And his plan is us."[15]

ALL PEOPLE ARE NOT CREATED EQUAL

I (Darren) once heard Andy Crouch give a talk on stewarding power and privilege. It opened my eyes to the staggering inequalities in the world. When it comes to earning an income there are four tiers of economic reality. The first is called wage.

Wage

I (Darren) got my first job when I was fourteen. I worked in a supermarket as a checkout operator. I clearly remember getting my very first paycheck. I had worked sixteen hours and I got six dollars an hour. At the age of fourteen I was so excited to be making all this money! The concept of a wage is that you do an hour's work and receive an hour's pay. You exchange your time for payment. This is a "wage." But there's something better; it's called rent.

Rent

The economic principle of "rent" is not referring to leasing a house. It's the idea of getting paid *more* for something that you would be willing to do for *less*. Take basketball star Kobe Bryant, for example. What if a talent agent was walking through a park one day and saw thirteen-year-old Kobe playing a pickup game of basketball? At thirteen, Kobe was probably already over six feet tall. What if this agent said, "Hey Kobe, do you like playing basketball? How would you like to get paid to play?"

Kobe would probably say, "That sounds great!"

"What if I pay you $10,000 per game for the rest of your life, how does that sound?"

Maybe young Kobe starts doing math in his head, if he has a fifteen-year career this could add up to millions of dollars. The reality is that today Kobe makes almost $300,000 per game. This doesn't include product endorsements and other sponsorships. But if Kobe was willing to play basketball for $10,000 per game and he started making $300,000 per game, then the difference, which is $290,000, is called "rent." It's the excess pay for what you would be willing to do for less. But in modern economics, there's an even better arrangement than this—it's called royalties.

Royalties

I (Darren) used to live in Nashville, Tennessee. Every restaurant was full of waiters and waitresses hoping to be discovered and become the next country music sensation. It was always strange to me that invariably they would spontaneously break out into song while walking around the restaurant, hoping a music industry executive would hear them and ask for a demo.

I had a friend who was a struggling musician. He wrote a song that was picked up by one of the biggest pop artists in the world. This song went on to be the most-often played song on American radio that year. Needless to say, my friend's life changed a little. You see, every single time his song was played on the radio he got paid. He only wrote the song once. It was only recorded once. But every time a radio station played it, or a movie soundtrack used it, or someone bought a CD, or downloaded it—he got paid. This is the wonder of earning "royalties." You do the work one time and then keep getting residual income. Would you believe there is something even better than earning royalties? There is. It's called privilege.

Privilege

Privilege is getting paid for doing nothing. It is getting paid just because of who you are. This is sometimes called the "Paris Hilton Effect." Privilege is receiving preferential treatment, favors, advantages, or money for something that you have done nothing to earn. It may be the way you look, the color of your skin, the family you were born into, or the place of your birth. Privilege is the way the world works.

When I (Jon) first moved to the United States, my student visa would not allow me to work outside of my college campus, so I joined the janitorial staff of my school in Texas. I worked throughout the summer with several other international students from Africa and Mexico. We cleaned bathrooms, mopped floors, vacuumed carpets, and emptied trash. One day it was over one hundred degrees and our team was hot and exhausted. We stopped in our break room where the international students on the janitorial team had their lunch. We had no air-conditioning and the vending machine held warm diet cokes for sale for one dollar apiece.

I was unassumingly sitting there eating a sandwich when one of the heads of the janitorial department came in and asked me to follow him. I followed him to another room that I had never seen before. It was another lunchroom! It was air-conditioned, nicely decorated, and drinks were free! I looked across the room and saw people talking, laughing, and generally enjoying themselves. The head janitor asked me to sit down and tell him stories about Australia. So I told him about my family and my life growing up. I don't think he had met an Aussie before, so for some reason he was just fascinated with my stories. He would laugh and gather others around to listen. I basically performed for these people.

After a few days of hanging in the nice lunchroom, I asked if I could bring some of my team to enjoy the air-conditioning, snacks, and drinks—they were in a steaming hot break room and would love this place.

"No," was the reply. "It doesn't work like that."

"But my friends are really hot in that other room."

"No, Jon, only you can come in here."

That was the first moment in my life when I realized I had privilege. I had no say over where I was born, the fact that this guy liked to listen to Australians talk, or that I had funny childhood stories that made this man laugh. I was getting preferential treatment, things handed to me, privilege—simply because of who I was.

THE GREENROOM

In many ways this is the concept of the "greenroom." A greenroom is a quiet room backstage reserved for VIPs only. It's usually filled with nice snacks, soft drinks, and coffee. A greenroom has a legitimate purpose. Musicians, artists, or speakers can gather their thoughts quietly before they go to serve the people. But if your desire is simply to isolate yourself and enjoy the benefits, you are exploiting it. You are looking for privilege, not service.

The apostle Paul said:

> *In your relationships with one another, have the same*
> *mindset as Christ Jesus:*
> *Who, being in very nature God,*
> > *did not consider equality with God something to*
> > > *be used to his own advantage;*
> *rather, he made himself nothing*
> > *by taking the very nature of a servant,*
> > *being made in human likeness.*
> *And being found in appearance as a man,*
> > *he humbled himself*
> > *by becoming obedient to death—*
> > > *even death on a cross!*[16]

It's probably safe to say that no one has ever had more privilege than God—the one who created everything. Jesus, who "did not consider equality with God something to be used to his own advantage" leveraged his privilege for others. If ever there was a greenroom, it was heaven. If ever someone stewarded his privilege, it was Jesus. The only person in all of human history who had the privilege to choose the time and circumstances of his birth, chose to come as a humble servant. He was born to an unwed teenage mother, to a despised racial minority, to show them their dignity, value, and worth before God.

Rather than using his privilege to have people serve him, Jesus came to serve and give his life as a ransom for many. The ongoing pattern of the Bible is that whenever God's people were given privilege, rather than squandering it on themselves, they were called steward it on behalf of the least and the forgotten.

When we compare ourselves to the rest of the world, we quickly find that we *live* in the greenroom. Our job is not simply to enjoy our quality of life, but to take the cultural advantage we have and work as advocates and activists on behalf of those on the underside of power. This is how the kingdom comes, on earth as it is in heaven.

WRENCHING PROBLEMS

Many years ago the leaders at Willow Creek became aware of a need for reliable transportation for single mothers so they could continue to provide for their families. Often these women were trying to maintain unreliable cars. Their cars would regularly break down, requiring repairs sometimes in the thousands of dollars. As we dug deeper into this issue, we discovered that when some single moms ended up homeless or found themselves in insurmountable debt, it could be traced back to their cars breaking down.

The domino effect trounced these women; often they were no longer able to take their children to childcare or to get to work.

The spiral continues. Finally, through no fault of their own, these mothers find themselves on the street looking for work and a place for their children to live.

We were not just trying to show compassion to these women in need, we were trying to address a deeper problem. We wanted to make sure these moms could hold on to their employment, maintain their income, and keep their dignity as the sole family provider. It seems like such a preventable reason for homelessness and poverty to take root. But many single moms wake up each morning and face this reality.

So our church started "C.A.R.S." (Christian Automotive Repairmen Serving). We take donations of any kind of vehicle, and our volunteer staff of more than one hundred serve in teams to restore the vehicles to fine working condition. The cars are then given to those in need of transportation—not least among them, single moms. Sometimes a person or family needs repairs to their own car but can't pay for them; we take care of that as well. When we steward our privilege, the kingdom comes.

Every week a team of attorneys from our church meets to advocate for the exploited and underprivileged. For most of the week these Chicago law firms focus on multimillion dollar corporate accounts, often defending frivolous lawsuits. But every

Tuesday these attorneys use their minds, education, and passion to lift up those who feel powerless and deeply discouraged. In just over one year, our legal aid ministry has served around nine hundred clients pro bono and our team has become one of the largest legal aid providers in Chicagoland. When we steward our privilege, the kingdom comes.

Charlotte was a physician's assistant working in a highly resourced hospital in an affluent suburb of Chicago. One day she felt challenged to be using her skills for the under-resourced. So Charlotte and her husband sold their home and bought a house in a low-income multiethnic neighborhood on the south side of the city. She joined the staff of a small under-resourced medical clinic in the neighborhood. Using her experience and contacts in the medical profession, Charlotte has dramatically upgraded the quality of health care that this community receives. When we steward our privilege, the kingdom comes.

My (Darren's) wife, Brandy, is a social worker. She grew up in an affluent environment in Nashville, Tennessee. Rather than pursuing the more lucrative family therapy option, she worked for the district attorney in the juvenile criminal justice system. She was an advocate for victims and their families. Her clients were primarily victims of violent crime and sex abuse from poor communities. Rather than advancing a career for herself, she lovingly guided people through a complex and often-harsh criminal justice system. Today Brandy works with single homeless mothers in a transitional housing program. When we steward our privilege, the kingdom comes.

A group of high school students learned about the biblical mandate of justice at our church. These teenagers attended one of the most highly resourced and highest rated public high schools in Illinois. One student did some research on education and discovered that there was a school on Chicago's south side that was so underfunded they didn't even have computers. Students were moving through their high school years with little or no opportunity to develop proficiencies in computer basics. This dumbfounded the teenagers in our church. So they pooled their money and raised more to fund a computer lab to be built in this school. Now students attending this south side school have an opportunity for the kind of education that could change the direction of their lives. When we steward our privilege, the kingdom comes.

Megan was so moved by the vision of living out justice that she went to college to become a water resource engineer. When she got married after she graduated, Megan and her new husband moved to Kenya to help try to solve the contaminated water crisis. When we steward our privilege, the kingdom comes.

Embedded in the symbol of our faith—the cross—are the solutions of our world. In one staggering act of stewarding privilege, God ushered in a movement of righteousness and justice, and we the church are called to join it today.

St. Teresa of Avila said this:

Christ has no body on earth but yours, no hands but yours, no feet but yours. Yours are the eyes through which Christ's compassion for the world is to look out; yours are the feet with which he is to go about doing good; and yours are the hands with which he is to bless us now.[17]

May we be the hands and feet of Jesus and transform these rumors of justice into reality in our world.

CHAPTER TEN

OUR BURNING REVOLUTION

Rumors of Hope

The modern mind is in complete disarray. Knowledge has stretched itself to the point where neither the world nor our intelligence can find any foot-hold. It is a fact that we are suffering from nihilism.

—Albert Camus

All that we call human history—money, poverty, ambition, war, prostitution, classes, empires, slavery—is the long terrible story of man trying to find something other than God which will make him happy.

—C. S. Lewis, *Mere Christianity*

May the God of hope fill you with all joy and peace as you trust in him, so that you may overflow with hope by the power of the Holy Spirit.

—the apostle Paul, to the Roman church

Seven miles from the city of Jerusalem was the small town of Emmaus. It's on the road there that we hear a remarkable story about God, about his heart, and about hope.

Three days after Jesus was executed at Calvary, just outside the walls of Jerusalem, two of his disciples were heading out of town. Although not part of the Twelve, for three years they followed Jesus and became increasingly convinced he was the Messiah. After all, Jesus had a compelling ministry of power and grace. He commanded the storm to stop, and it did. He cleansed people with leprosy. He healed the blind and the deaf. He confronted the religious hypocrisy of his day. His teaching brought illumination and insight to the Scriptures and made God's kingdom seem near.

Then things went terribly wrong. The man they had set their hopes on died. Not just a normal death, but a defeat at the hands of their oppressors, the Romans. Imagine how the disciples felt—they had followed Jesus for three years. And now, on the road to Emmaus, they were replaying everything that had happened. Slowly but surely, cynicism entered their hearts. God had forgotten them. He was absent, distant, and they were walking away.

As a culture, we can relate to how these disciples felt. God often seems absent, distant, as if he has walked away. As a result, cynicism has filled our hearts. Some of it is the low-grade kind—a subtle arrogance about the questions our generation seems to be asking. Then there's the dangerous kind, a cynicism of the soul that dares to look God in the eye with an arrogant belief that we could do a better job of running the world than he does.

Cynicism has permeated our world. It seems to have infected everything. From the media we watch, to the institutions we see crumble before us, to the families we grow up in, to the atrocities in our day. The true test, however, of how far we have fallen into cynicism can only be found in the stories we tell our children.

LIFE AFTER GOD

In his book *Life After God*, Douglas Coupland tells a series of stories to pacify his child who has lost her favorite Dr. Seuss book.

We stayed at a motel in Kamloops that night, halfway to our ultimate destination. I just couldn't make it any further. After we got settled into our room, the big drama was that we forgot your Dr. Seuss book back at the Chicken Shack in Merritt. You refused to settle down until I told you a story and so I was forced to improvise in spite of my tiredness, something I am not good at doing. And so out of nowhere, I just said what came into my head and I told you the story of "Doggles."

"Doggles?" you asked.

"Yes—Doggles—the dog who wore goggles."

And then you asked me what did Doggles do, and I couldn't think of anything else aside from the fact that he wore goggles.

You persisted and so I said to you, "Well, Doggles was supposed to have a starring role in the Cat in the Hat series of books except . . ."

"Except what?" you asked.

"Except he had a drinking problem," I replied.

"Just like Grandpa," you said, pleased to be able to make a real life connection.

"I suppose so," I said.

So then you wanted to hear about another animal, and so I asked you if you'd ever heard of Squirrelly the Squirrel, and you said you hadn't. So I said, "Well Squirrelly was going to have an exhibition of nut paintings at the Vancouver Art Gallery except . . ."

"Except what?" you asked.

"Except Mrs. Squirrelly had baby squirrels and so Squirrelly had to get a job at the peanut butter factory and was never able to finish his work."

"Oh."

I paused. "You want to hear about any other animals?"

"Uh, I guess so," you replied, a bit ambiguously.

"Did you ever hear of Clappy the Kitten?"

"No."

"Well, Clappy the Kitten was going to be a movie star one day. But then she rang up too many bills on her MasterCard and had to get a job as a teller at the Hong Kong Bank of Canada to pay them off. Before long she was simply too old to try becoming a star—or her ambition disappeared—or both. And she found it was easier to just talk about doing it instead of actually doing it and . . ."

"And what?" you asked.

"Nothing, baby," I said, stopping myself then and there—feeling suddenly more dreadful than you can imagine having told you about these animals—filling your head with these stories—stories of these beautiful little creatures who were all supposed to have been part of a fairy tale but who got lost along the way.[1]

Those last words sum up the angst of an entire generation: "Beautiful little creatures who were all supposed to have been part of a fairy tale but who got lost along the way."

It's one thing for hopelessness to exist in the world, but when it makes its way into the church, a crisis ensues. We meet an increasing number of people who seem to have gotten lost along the way. Lost through sin, shame, hypocrisy, abuse, or just plain rebellion. Many people are despondent about the future and have resigned their stories to a sort of heartless fatalism, which in itself is fatal for people who claim to follow Jesus.

When life teems with brokenness, poverty, disappointment, greed, divorce, and pain, Christians, as frequently as anyone, seem to struggle to figure out how to live with hope. How do we maintain faith in a God who writes poetic promises in the Scriptures, yet leaves the threads of our own stories frayed and ragged at the edges?

I have often wondered how Jesus' disciples processed hope in the midst of their own experience. The movement of Jesus looked nothing like they had originally envisioned. How did they move from the cynicism and fear at the end of the Gospels, to the church we see in the book of Acts?

EASTERTIDE

There is a little section in the Scriptures that in many ways articulates the time of history in which we live. It shows how God responds to those wrestling with hopelessness and cynicism. It's found in the last few chapters of the Gospels and celebrated in the traditional church calendar as the season of Eastertide. Eastertide is the fifty-day period between Jesus' resurrection and Pentecost Sunday, where Jesus has just a few short days to lay the foundations of his church before he returns to his Father.

Pause for a moment and ask yourself this question. If you were the resurrected Son of God, who had just overcome death and hell, how would you spend these fifty days? If you had a resurrected body, how would you use it to establish your reign before ascending to the right hand of the Father?

Perhaps Jesus should have gone to Rome, fought in the Coliseum, worked his way up to a face-to-face showdown with Caesar, gladiator-style, and won the masses with his power and might. Or maybe Jesus should have confronted the Jewish leaders who crucified him, dismantled their corrupt system, set up his headquarters in Jerusalem, and ushered in the kingdom of God. That's what we would have done.

But that's not what Jesus did. And what he did do during his last forty days reveals something amazing about the heart of God.

He doesn't build his movement on the praise of the crowds, the wisdom of the scholars, the might of the army, or access to the cultural elites. Jesus spends his time finding his followers who were lost in the fallout between his death and resurrection, and he goes about lovingly, convincingly, restoring their hope.

Acts 1:3 puts it like this: "After his suffering, he showed himself to these men and gave many convincing proofs that he was alive. He appeared to them over a period of forty days and spoke about the kingdom of God"(NIV 1984).

He appeared, showed, convinced, and spoke about the kingdom of God. Apparently this is what Jesus did to lay a foundation for a church that would last thousands of years. He made sure that those beautiful creatures who got lost along the way recovered their place in the story God was telling.

THE ROAD TO EMMAUS

One of the most personal and moving of these encounters is found in Luke 24. It takes place on one of the small dusty roads that makes its way out of the city of Jerusalem.

Despite rumors of Jesus' resurrection, two of his followers, disappointed in the kind of messiah he turned out to be, were leaving the city. But who were these disciples? We know they were associated with the apostles and they were a part of Jesus' inner core. On the road to Emmaus they commented that some of "our women" came to them this morning with a vision of angels and rumors that he was alive. And we know one of the disciples was named Cleopas.

In John's Gospel we read that at the scene of Jesus' crucifixion one of the women standing there was Mary, the wife of Clopas.[2] Some scholars believe Clopas and Cleopas are the same person. Could it be that the two disciples on the road to Emmaus were Clopas and his wife, Mary, leaving the city because their messiah had failed?

It seems that in spite of their relational connection to the disciples, proximity to Jesus, and even rumors that he was back from the dead, they had abandoned hope and were headed to Emmaus.

As they were leaving Jerusalem, and leaving the movement of Jesus, Jesus himself walked with them. Now here is a revelation of God's heart: Jesus walking with the disillusioned as they are walking away from him.

"What are you discussing together as you walk along?" [Jesus asked.]

They stood still, their faces downcast. One of them, named Cleopas, asked him, "Are you [only a visitor] to Jerusalem [and do not] know the things that have happened there in these days?"

"What things?" he asked.

"About Jesus of Nazareth," they replied. "He was a prophet, powerful in word and deed before God and all the people. The chief priests and our rulers handed him over to be sentenced to death, and they crucified him; but we had hoped that he was the one who was going to redeem Israel."[3]

But We Had Hoped

In these few short words, in our hearts we hear the pain and disappointment of many. They had hoped that Jesus was *the* Messiah, that he would redeem Israel, that God's kingdom would be fully manifest, and so would their hopes. It didn't turn out this way. Mary was there at the foot of the cross, watching Jesus' "defeat" at the hands of the Romans. Crucifixion was a political punishment, a graphic and forcible reminder that Rome had won, and you had lost. And here was their failed Messiah, hanging on a cross, along with the hopes of a young Jewish couple, looking for a revolution. So what sort of Messiah did they hope for?

Mighty in Word and Deed

Since Moses' prophetic claim, that one mightier than he would rise, the children of Israel had been waiting for the Messiah. With the rise of King David and Israel's golden age, their hopes only increased that they would recover their land and their kingdom.

They had been tossed to and fro by the rising tides of nations and empires, sometimes faring better than others, all the while tenaciously clinging to their covenant and hope. After the fall of Alexander the Great, the known world was split between four of his generals. The Greeks were committed to spreading their culture. When confronted with the Jews, who believed their culture was God-given, it was inevitable that conflict would arise.

In the year 167 BC, Antiochus IV Epiphanes tried to force the Jewish people to submit to Greek culture. He ordered the high priest to defile the temple by sacrificing a pig in the Holy of Holies. For the Jewish people, this was unthinkable. At the last minute the Jewish priest Mattathias rose up and killed the priest before he could commit this blasphemous act. This started a full-blown rebellion. Mattathias was eventually killed in battle, and the following year his son, Judas Maccabeus, continued the resistance. Known in history as "the Hammer," Judas Maccabeus led a guerilla war that resulted in a stunning military victory. His fame and legend rose, and he was known as a heroic leader, mighty in word and deed. The most famous moment in the Hammer's career was a surprise attack he launched on a group of unsuspecting generals. It was a definitive success. This battle is considered by many to be one of the fifty pivotal battles in history. It was the turning point that enabled Jewish independence.

Like a scene from *Braveheart*, Maccabeus used the following words to inspire his men. He told them that "they ought to fight, though it were with their naked bodies, for that God had sometimes of old given such men strength, and that against such as were more in number, and were armed also, out of regard to their great courage."

He commanded the trumpeters to sound for the battle: "For it is better for us to die in battle than to see the evils of our nation, and of the holies. Nevertheless, as it shall be the will of God in heaven, so be it done."⁴

Judas Maccabeus was known as a mighty leader, powerful in word and deed. He restored the Israelites to their covenant land, destroyed the opposing forces, set the captives free, and cleansed and rededicated the temple.

If you were a young Jewish couple, thinking about a revolution, your last cultural memory of someone who had actually succeeded was Judas "the Hammer" Maccabeus.

Rumors of a Messiah

First century Jews cherished Judas Maccabeus.

Now imagine what would have begun to stir in your heart when you first heard the rumors about Jesus.

> Jesus' first message was "Repent, because the kingdom of God is at hand."

> Jesus' first public sermon stated that he had come to set the captives free.

> Jesus taught with authority and had a reputation of being mighty in word and deed.

> Jesus taught the heart of the Torah and came to fulfill God's promises to his people.

> Jesus confronted the hypocrisy of the religious leaders and cleansed the temple.

Now imagine what would have happened when he invited people to come and follow him. What would be going through their minds? What was being stirred from their cultural consciousness that ignited hope in their hearts? Imagine following Jesus and seeing the crowds and his miraculous power grow. Imagine giving your life to a leader who was determined to go to the capital of their world, and usher in the kingdom of God. I am sure that the Jews hearing and watching Jesus were on the edge of their seats, hoping and believing that this could indeed be the Messiah.

Then, almost as if in slow motion, it begins to unravel. Jesus is betrayed by a friend, tried and convicted, and he doesn't fight back. One of his disciples pulls out a sword, only to have Jesus heal the man who is injured by it. Jesus is mocked, marched through the streets of Jerusalem, and crucified on a hill overlooking the city—a city he had failed to save.

And then you have Mary, the wife of Clopas, sitting at the foot of the cross, praying against hope that something miraculous is going to happen. But it doesn't. He dies. Hope dies. And the Romans win the day.

I can't help but think what must have been going through the minds of these disciples as they headed to Emmaus. While walking along, they encountered a stranger, who drew out their thoughts.

"He was a prophet, powerful in word and deed before God and all the people. The chief priests and our rulers handed him over to be sentenced to death, and they crucified him; but we had hoped that he was the one who was going to redeem Israel."[5]

"But we had hoped" is often the reason many of us decide to take the road to Emmaus. We live with a continuous stream of messages that tell us the Christian life is easy—God exists to meet our expectations, conform to our will, and act in a way that we think is best. But it doesn't always work like that.

Emmaus

A young couple leaves the movement of Jesus and heads to the village of Emmaus. But of all the places they could go, why *Emmaus*? Why trade Jerusalem for *this* small town?

Why would they be searching for hope there?

Remember the great military victory of Judas Maccabeus? The one with the *Braveheart*-esque speech? The turning point in Jewish independence? That victory happened in the village of Emmaus.

Is it possible that these disciples, walking away from Jerusalem, were walking to Emmaus, because that was the last place God powerfully moved? Maybe they were heading to Emmaus, because when Jesus failed, they were looking for another Maccabeus.

Maybe you are on your own road to Emmaus.

Perhaps your marriage is a disappointment. Maybe your ministry has been a failure. Maybe a loved one has died. Maybe you're single and desperately lonely. Maybe your child is far from God. Maybe you are wrestling with a major illness.

At some point we have all breathed what Radiohead calls "The Universal Sigh." We have all left Jerusalem. We have all lost our hope.

Concerning Himself

"Did not the Messiah have to suffer these things and then enter his glory?" And beginning with Moses and all the Prophets, he explained to them what was said in all the Scriptures concerning himself.[6]

So why is Jesus going after *them*? Why bother with two cynics who were walking away? Because of love; Jesus is compelled by love. He still leaves the ninety-nine to find the one. He searches the house until he finds the coin. He hosts the party for the return of the prodigal. Jesus believes that despair is not the final word. Jesus' love propels him to rescue us from our smaller stories and reunite us to his. Because for the one who came to seek and save the lost, hope is not a myth. The story of the Scriptures is the story of Jesus. Hope is not concerning our circumstances. Hope is concerning Jesus.

WHEN HOPE IS GONE

Josh was a pastor who made a mistake. The stress, complexity, and criticism that came with leading his church had become exhausting and overwhelming. He needed an escape. The escape hatch that he chose was to disappear into a fantasy world of online pornography. One day when his administrative assistant was checking something on his computer, she accidently discovered a world that he had hidden from his wife, family, and the church.

The way the lay leadership decided to handle this was devastating. As Josh was getting ready to step up to preach, a lay leader asked if he could quickly say a few words. Completely surprised and unprepared, Josh smiled and said, "Sure, go ahead."

This man proceeded to share that the leadership of the church had made a disgusting discovery about Pastor Josh that week. He went on to explain that the sin of pornography addiction had to be made public and that Josh's position was terminated effective immediately. Josh looked at his wife and his seven-year-old daughter who were also in the room. The whole church sat in silence; Josh stood up and walked out of the building. That was the last time he'd ever step foot in the church.

Josh lost his job, his church, his friends, his reputation, and relationships with his family were strained. Josh fell into deep depression. He even considered taking his own life. Just to make ends meet he started working two jobs. One was as an overnight security guard at an office building and the other was as a waiter in a restaurant.

Eighteen months passed. Lynne, a woman who had attended Josh's former church, began asking about what he was doing now. She heard a rumor that he was waiting tables at a restaurant in a nearby area, but no one knew which one. Lynne went from restaurant to restaurant determined to find Josh.

After two months of making her way through different restaurants, she saw a man who looked like him. She called out to him and he looked up.

"Can I talk to you?" She asked.

He wiped his hands and walked toward her.

"Yes?" he hesitantly responded.

"Josh, do you remember me? I was a part of your church."

Josh's head dropped. She continued.

"I have a message for you."

Josh lifted his eyes.

"Josh, God is not done with you yet! This is not the final scene in your life. God wants to restore you and use your story to show others his grace."

She handed Josh a check.

"This is an investment in your future church."

Over a period of months, Josh walked through a process of restoration and eventually started another church. This church is defined as a place where people who have lost their way are greeted with love and grace. Lynne embodied the spirit of Jesus, a

God who comes after us and won't rest or settle until we recover our place in the story he is telling.

OUR BURNING HEARTS

Josh could relate to the disciples walking to Emmaus. Something happened in his heart, just as it did in theirs. "Were not our hearts burning?" they asked. When people are discouraged or disappointed or feeling a sense of shame, they need God to restore something in their hearts.

We become a light against the cynicism of our culture.

We as a culture have come to the end of ourselves; we have lost our context, our story, our place in the grander scheme of things. It is into this aching world that Jesus sent his disciples. They were restored and burning with a message of a suffering and glorified King.

After the two disciples on the road to Emmaus pleaded with Jesus to have dinner with them, something beautiful happened. Jesus revealed his true identity when he broke bread with them, one of the most intimate moments friends could share in the ancient Middle East. Jesus ultimately gave his followers more than just the gift of restored hope and a recovered story—he gave them himself. Ultimately it's an encounter with Jesus that will restore hope to our cynical hearts.

And the resurrected Jesus is still on the road, finding all sorts of beautiful creatures who have been lost along the way. I'm convinced that one of the reasons Jesus didn't confront the might of Rome or challenge the religious powers in Jerusalem was because he knew the story we long to hear is not one of military victory or political control. It's the story of a God who restores the lost and offers hope to a cynical world.

The rumors of God are true. Jesus rose from the dead, and so did the hopes of all those who are looking for a revolution. The statues are coming to life.

EPILOGUE

In Our Day

In 1857 churches all over New York City were noticing a sharp decline in church membership. One Dutch Reformed church that met on Fulton Street in Lower Manhattan saw a surprising drop in attendance. So a meeting was called with church leaders to discuss this recent trend. A lay leader named Jeremiah Lanphier, a local businessman, was commissioned to start a prayer meeting during his lunch hour. Lanphier began promoting his noonday prayer meeting to surrounding businesses. He prepared a printed handout that read:

> A day of Prayer-Meeting is held every Wednesday from 12 to 1 o'clock in the Consistory building in the rear of the North Dutch Church, corner of Fulton and William Streets. This meeting is intended to give merchants, mechanics, clerks, strangers and businessmen generally an opportunity to stop and call on God amid the perplexities incident to their respective avocations. It will continue for one hour.[1]

On Wednesday, September 21, 1857, he showed up to pray at noon. He prayed alone for the first thirty minutes and then another businessman joined him. By 1:00 p.m. six men were quietly praying. The following Wednesday twenty people gathered, the next week almost forty people came to pray at noon. After several weeks the prayer gatherings changed from weekly to daily, then they outgrew the church building on Fulton Street.

Inspired by Lanphier's simple vision, the Plymouth Church in Brooklyn also began daily prayer meetings at noon. Within months noonday prayer meetings sprang up in Dutch Reformed, Presbyterian, Congregational, Methodist, and Episcopal churches all over the city. Thousands of people started to gather in churches at noon to pray. Many factories began blowing their lunch whistle at 11:55 a.m. to give their employees time to make it to a church by noon to pray.

One day at a few minutes before twelve, a senior editor of a newspaper was looking out of his window and was shocked to see people running from their places of business, bumping into one another, yet within minutes they had all disappeared into churches. He sent a reporter down to investigate, who returned with the astonishing report: "They're all praying!"

By 1858 the *New York Herald* and *The New York Tribune* were both running regular columns on the "Noonday Prayer Meetings." It was reported that as many as forty thousand people were praying across the city. The *New York Times* called it "the most remarkable movement since the Reformation."

This noonday prayer movement began to spread across America—in Denver, Cleveland, Los Angeles, and Chicago, noonday prayer meetings began to emerge. Most church historians agree that by 1859 more than one million unchurched Americans had become Christians. At that point the population was only thirty million people. With the current population now ten times that figure, it would be the equivalent of more than ten million people becoming followers of Jesus today.[2]

The United States has a history of the unmistakable activity of God. Does God still move like this today?

In other parts of the world, God is moving in breathtaking power. The life of God is not just a rumor to them; it is the reality they live in day by day.

The underground church in China is seeing growth that may rival the growth in the book of Acts.

In Central America, churches unite across cities for whole nights of prayer and worship.

In Africa, entire countries are having their hearts stirred to turn back to God.

Even in frigid Europe, there are signs and rumblings of the fresh work of God.

But what about us? Are we simply content to watch the American church limp into eternity? Are you ready to drift through the rest of your life, lulled and softened by our comfort and ease? We believe that deep in your soul you long to see the fame and deeds of God renewed and known in our time. We believe that you were created for a radical pursuit of Jesus and his kingdom.

The rumors of the fame and deeds of God are true. We believe he rewards those who earnestly seek him. Frederick B. Meyer famously said, "The great tragedy of life is not unanswered prayer but unoffered prayer."

May we be among those who believe that the greatest days of the church are still to come.

May we ask, seek, and knock for the kingdom to break into our lives.

And may we echo the prayer of the prophet Habakkuk:

> LORD, *I have heard of your fame;*
> *I stand in awe of your deeds,* LORD.
> *Renew them in our day,*
> *in our time make them known;*
> *in wrath remember mercy.*[3]

ABOUT THE AUTHORS

Jon Tyson is the pastor of Trinity Grace Church in New York City. Originally from Australia, Jon moved to the United States fourteen years ago with a passion to understand and help work out the future of the Western church. He lives, works, and serves in one of the largest cultural and missionary contexts of the world— the global city. Trinity Grace has five churches in New York. Jon is also on the board of City Collective, a network of incarnational churches committed to multiplying missional church networks in the urban centers of the world. He lives in Manhattan with his wife, Christy, and their two children. You can see more about their church at www.trinitygracechurch.com and the network at www.citycollective.org.

—

Originally from Australia, Darren Whitehead has lived in the United States for more than thirteen years. With a passion for the global church, Darren joined the staff of one of the most influential churches in North America—Willow Creek Community Church. As teaching pastor, Darren and senior pastor Bill Hybels share the weekend service teaching responsibilities for all six campuses. Darren lives with his wife, Brandy, and their three daughters just outside of Chicago, Illinois. For more information about Willow Creek go to www.willowcreek.org.

ACKNOWLEDGMENTS

Book acknowledgments are a little like movie credits; you only read them if your name is mentioned. So if you bother to read this, you probably heard you got a shout out!

DARREN'S THANKS:

Jesus, I am stunned that you called me out of darkness into your marvelous light.

Brandy, we grew up on opposite sides of the world, and I could never have known the rich companionship that you would bring into my life. Thanks for your love, kindness, honesty, belief, and support. The best is yet to come.

Sydney, Scarlett, and Violet, the love and affection I feel toward you can only be expressed in long snuggles. May Jesus be your hope and may you each discover that the rumors are true.

Mum, you lived in a home with four boys; now I live in a home with four girls. I pray I will show them the same love, truth, and grace you showed us.

Dad, you are the real deal. The most sincere and authentic person I know. George and Jeanna, thanks for your huge love and support, and thanks for raising an amazing daughter.

Reece and Steph, so excited that we can raise our kids together. Here's to living the dream. Grant and Bev, thanks for your love and support. I'm inspired by how you live out your convictions. Graeme Smith, I still remember the words you spoke to me when I was thirteen years old. Thanks for allowing God to speak through you at the most defining times of my life. Tom Yeats, you were the first person I saw truly captured by Jesus. Mark Elmendorp, I will never forget the intentional investment you made in me.

Ashley and Russell Evans, thanks for giving me a vision for the kingdom and the world. Martyn Manuel, Kakadu, Sydney, and the "Albies" changed my life. Dan Crinion, hello and welcome to the show. Thwop! Tanya, Trudy, Ingrid, and Corinne, God has his hand on each of you. Cameron Bennett, your vision, passion, and faithfulness are inspiring. Ben Fewster, who'd a thought a trip to the U.S. would change so much?

Dave, Helen, Rebecca, Daniel, Ben, Joel, Luke, Josh, and Libby Smallbone, thanks for opening your hearts and your home (aka Nashville's Australian Embassy). God used you all to dramatically change the direction of my life. Zach Kelm, what a golden era of our lives! Matt (Austin) Shuff, thanks for the wisdom you shared at the Coffee Beanery. Brian Payne, "Y'all are welcome to stay." Your hunger for the Scriptures is contagious. Duane Ward, thanks for believing in me—and always taking my calls when I'm seeking wisdom.

Rick White, thanks for giving me my first opportunity to preach at a church. I am so grateful. Diane Cobb, The Steps of Faith. God of the "Thus Far." You are one of kind. You have left an indelible mark on my life. And that's all I know.

Don Sapaugh, thanks for asking me some of the most definitive questions of my life. Mike Breaux, thanks for calling me. Gene Appel, thanks for your unlimited encouragement. Bill Hybels, no other leader has invested more specifically and intentionally in me than you. It is such an honor. Paul and Deirdre, Shane and Wendy, Aaron and Shauna, Brian and Jorie, Jon and Kelly, Matt and Kristi, Jon and Maria, Jake and Alison, doing life together is as good as it gets. Bryan and Steph Jones—Bryan, I am proud of the man of God you are. Steph, you are family to us.

To the best team I have ever been a part of—the Willow Creek Leadership Team: Bill Hybels, Pat Cimo, Leanne Mellado, Ted Allen Miller, Brian McAuliffe, Heather Larson, Colby Burke, and Greg Hawkins.

To the most amazing church in the world—Willow Creek Community Church. Your faith inspires me. Your generosity amazes me and your vision compels me. Thanks for letting an Aussie in.

JON'S THANKS:

God. I want to be the one leper you heal who comes back to thank you. The whole thing is a gift. Maranatha.

Christy. Here's to long weekends in Europe in our forties.

Nate. Thanks for letting me write this book. I owe you some paintball in the woods.

Haley. You are an endless source of delight. Let's do tea.

Mum and Dad. Thanks for believing in me from day one. Thanks for maxing out your Visa so I could come to America, and for the prayers of protection.

Cathy. Thanks for letting your brother live on the other side of the world, and not complaining about it too often.

Dick, Diane, Patty. My American family. Thanks for taking me in, and being more than generous.

Russell Evans. The first one to tell me that the rumors of God were true.

Paul Geerling. For modeling preposterous faith.

Jeff Spencer. Your investment in my life has had an incalculable impact. Your vision of discipleship has been present in all I do. Cheers.

Rick White. Thanks for taking a risk on a twenty-three-year-old kid, and being one of the most generous men I know. You've got my respect.

Diane Cobb. You are the one who taught me how to love. I'm just crazy about you.

To the finest people I know. My church family at Trinity Grace. Thank you for seeing "in New York as it is in heaven."

Billy and Kelly Patterson. Thanks for pointing out how I was well on my way to wasting my life. You spurred this into being.

Josh and Jess Staton. For carrying an insurmountable burden at a ridiculously young age. With joy.

Rickey Kraemer. For being a part of *our* story, and learning how to tell *the* story better than anyone I know. And for getting your wife. Well done.

Patrick and Teresa Murphy. Thank you for sticking it out. For going all in again and again, and forgiving me of the biggest leadership mistakes of my life. I'm sincerely grateful.

Mike and Beatrix Tafoya. By the grace of God, you have the finest character I know. Thanks for seeing me through the eyes of faith. It's been a privilege doing this with you.

Gary and Charlotte. You are the literal answers to prayers that we prayed on the roof of the old office in midtown Manhattan. I would not want to do this without you.

Alf and Tanya. Thanks for paying the price to "do it differently." Alf, you are the "duke of community."

Sue-Bird. Thank you, thank you, thank you for organizing my life. You put up with my idiosyncrasies with much grace. Everyone repeat after me, "Sue actually runs the church."

Caleb and Alison Clardy. For assuring me that the vision of "bringing the kingdom of God, in the world's most brilliant city, with people you love," was something others wanted to join. Spread love, it's the Brooklyn way.

Zach and Stacy Williams. For modeling grace. And leading us to the throne as only you can.

James Cernero. How far have you come since our first coffee? Good on ya, mate.

K. Ball. For running the borough of Brooklyn, with love.

Guy and Rebecca Wasko. For believing in your gut that "we get to be a part of this."

Tyler. For raising a generation of church planters who aren't white.

Eric and Emily Marshall. For giving voice to the beautiful thing we are trying to do here.

Won and Caroline Kim. You *are* marrow.

Suzy Silk. For weeping over Jerusalem, and New York.

Jessica Joy. You are a church planter in the truest sense of the term. There will be a great reward for you.

Joelle. For "getting it" before almost anyone else.

Bill Kerr. What God has done in you is astounding. Claim your inheritance.

Ted. I am more proud of you than ever. Isaiah 58.

Jean-Michelle. For believing deep in your soul.

Greg Wong. Thanks for investing your gifts and not burying them in the ground. May God give you more influence as a result.

Steve Hoppe. You have an iron chin. Your service to our

church has been amazing. Thank you.

Ray East. For fanning into flame the gifts of God within us all.

Kasey Taylor. A man in full.

Trish Horst. For weeping that day at our house, and making the move to the city.

And to the leadership community of TGC. You make life worth living. Your passion for God and compassion for people are second to none. Thank you for embodying the way of Jesus, and following hard after God. I cannot wait to see the fame and deeds of God, renewed and known in our time.

SPECIAL THANKS

Shauna Niequist, your insights and feedback were brilliant. Bill Hybels, thanks for your support and for writing the Foreword. Brandon Grissom, Heather Larson, Aaron Niequist, thanks for your encouragement and feedback. Brad Lomenick, for believing we should write the book. You're a legend. Susan Delay, thanks for your amazing help. Tim Willard, thanks for your long hours and insightful thoughts.

Mike Smallbone, thanks for your vision for this project and your huge investment of wisdom and advice.

Scot McKnight, your wisdom and feedback had a huge impact on the direction of this book.

Glenn Lucke, thanks for your insightful feedback and encouragement.

Kristen Parrish, for taking a risk on us. You are wonderful. The rest of the Thomas Nelson crew. Thank you so much.

NOTES

Chapter One

Epigraph—Habakkuk 3:2 TNIV.

1. C. S. Lewis, *Mere Christianity* (San Francisco: Harper, 1980), 87.

2. John 10:10 NKJV.

3. Kosman, Mayer, and Keysar, American Religious Identification Survey, 2001, http://www.gc.cuny.edu/faculty/research_briefs/aris.pdf (accessed February 11, 2011).

4. See epigraph.

Chapter Two

Epigraph—The apostle Paul: Ephesians 3:20 NIV.

1. Kalle Lasn, *Culture Jam: The Uncooling of America* (New York: Eagle Brook, 1999), xiii. We first read this quote in *Colossians Remixed* by Brian J. Walsh and Sylvia C. Keesmaat (Downers Grove, IL: IVP Academic), 170–171, and are thankful for the language of *Colossians Remixed*.

2. Neil Gabler, *Walt Disney: The Triumph of the American Imagination* (Vintage Books, 2006), xv. Thanks to Mark Sayers for exposing me (Darren) to Neil Gabler's insightful writing.

3. McDonald's/Stanford University Medical School study, 20.

4. Sally Hogshead, "Fascinate: Your 7 Triggers to Persuasion and Captivation," *Harper Business*, first printing edition (February 9, 2010).

5. Ann Hulbert, "Tweens 'R' Us," *The New York Times*, November 28, 2004.

6. "Television Advertising Leads to Unhealthy Habits in Children, Says APA Task Force," American Psychological Association, February 23, 2004.

7. "Children, Adolescents, and Advertising," *Journal of the American Academy of Pediatrics*, 2006, 2563. http://www.media-awareness. ca/english/parents/marketing/advertising_everywhere.cfm (accessed February 11, 2011).

8. Matthew 7:9–11 NIV.

9. C. S. Lewis, *Weight of Glory* (preached originally as a sermon in the Church of St. Mary the Virgin, Oxford, on June 8, 1942: published in *Theology*, November 1941, and by the S.P.C.K, 1942).

10. James 4:2 NIV.

11. James 4:3 NIV.

12. Matthew 6:10–11, paraphrased.

13. Colossians 3:1–2.

14. Acts 2:17 NIV.

15. Hebrews 11:6 NIV.

Chapter Three

Epigraph—Hebrews 13:5 NIV.

1. Steve Wieberg, "Analysts: Bronze medal leads to more happiness than silver," *USA Today*, February 22, 2010. http://www. usatoday.com/sports/olympics/vancouver/2010-02-22-bronze-vs-silver_N.htm (accessed February 13, 2011).

2. John Wiley & Sons, Inc., 2009; 1.

3. Statistics found at http://www.worldwatercouncil.org/index. php?id=23 (accessed February 13, 2011).

4. Matthew 6:25, 31–33 NIV.

5. 1 Timothy 6:17 NIV.

6. 1 Timothy 6:18–19 NIV.

7. Victor Lebow, "Price of Competition in 1955," *Jounal of Retailing*, Spring 1955, Vol. XXXI, No. 1, 5.

8. Annie Leonard, *The Story of Stuff* (Free Press, 2010).

9. For a somewhat complicated read of Derrida's concept of the gift, read chapter 1 of *Rethinking God as Gift: Marion, Derrida, and the Limits of Phenomenology* (Perspectives in Continental Philosophy). Robyn Horner, Fordham University Press; 4th edition (July 1, 2001).

10. Matthew 6:1–3 NIV.

11. Acts 4:32–35 NIV.

12. 1 John 3:14, 16–18 NIV.

13. 1 Corinthians 13:3 NIV.

14. 2 Corinthians 8:9 NIV.

15. Luke 12:15–21 NIV.

16. Philippians 1:21 NIV.

17. Luke 12:15; 1 Timothy 6:19.

18. Brad J. Kallenberg, *Live to Tell: Evangelism for a Postmodern Age.* Brazos Press (November 1, 2002).

Chapter Four

Epigraph—The beloved apostle John: 1 John 4:19 KJV.

1. Donald Miller, http://en.wikiquote.org/wiki/Don_Miller_ (author) (accessed February 15, 2011).

2. Revelation 2:2 NIV.

3. Revelation 2:4–5 NIV.

4. Paul wrote the letters of 1 and 2 Timothy to Timothy, who was leading the church at Ephesus.

5. It's also an accepted theory that several congregations constituted the Ephesian church. So that instead of just one specific church, the Ephesian church represented a regional body of believers.

6. Acts 19:11–12 NIV.

7. Acts 19:17–20 NIV.

8. Acts 19:8–10 NIV.

9. Ephesians 2:6 NIV

10. Revelation 2:5 NIV.

11. Ephesians 3:17–19 NIV.

12. Matthew 3:16–17 NIV.

13. Ephesians 3:20–21 NIV.

Chapter Five

Epigraph—The apostle Paul: Romans 5:20–21 NIV 2011.

1. Luke 15:7.

2. Ephesians 2:1–3 NIV 1984.

3. Ephesians 1:18.

4. I first heard Tim Keller explain the sinful nature this way, as a "coping mechanism for life without God."

5. Ephesians 2:4–9 NIV 1984.

6. John 3:17.

7. Ephesians 2:8.

8. I heard Bill Johnston say this in a passing comment, and it forever changed my view of ministry.

9. Romans 2:4 NIV.

10. 1 John 1:9.

Chapter Six

Epigraphs—C. S. Lewis, *Mere Christianity* (New York: Macmillan, 1952), 104; the apostle Paul: Colossians 3:13 NIV 2011.

1. Colossians 3:13 NIV.

2. Jonah 3:4 NIV.

3. Jonah 4:1 NIV 1984.

4. Jonah 4:2–3 NIV 1984.

5. Judgment at Nineveh Podcast, www.dancarlin.com, published Friday, December 14, 2007.

6. Albert Schweitzer. Great-Quotes.com, Gledhill Enterprises, 2011. http://www.great-quotes.com/quote/33081 (accessed February 13, 2011).

7. Martin Luther King Jr., BrainyQuote.com, Xplore Inc., 2011. http://www.brainyquote.com/quotes/quotes/m/martinluth 101472.html (accessed February 13, 2011).

8. Isaiah 55:6–9 NIV.

9. Jonah 4:3 NIV.

Chapter Seven

Epigraph—The apostle Paul: 1 Corinthians 12:21 NKJV.

1. Mark Sayers is the author of two books: *The Trouble with Paris* (Nashville: Thomas Nelson, 2008) and *Vertical Self* (Nashville: Thomas Nelson, 2010). Both books come with our highest recommendation. His blog (www.marksayers.wordpress.com) is also a great resource and cultural commentary.

2. *New York Art World Magazine*, Commentary, http://www. newyorkartworld.com/commentary/holland2.html (accessed February 11, 2011).

3. Matthew 16:25 NIV; Luke 14:26 NASB.

4. http://www.associatedcontent.com/article/154012/man_dies_
in_front_of_tv_and_no_one.html.

5. Will Kelley continued to battle Leukemia until May 22, 2010,
when he was welcomed into eternity by Jesus. The way Will
lived and loved continues to inspire many people today including
my (Darren's) own family. We will see you again, but until that
"faithful" day—peace in the midst.

Chapter Eight

Epigraph—The apostle Peter: 1 Peter 4:8 NIV.

1. The character Rose Walker in *The Sandman* #65, later
republished in *The Sandman Volume 9: The Kindly Ones,* part 9,
7–8, 1996, Vertigo.

2. Alain de Botton, *Status Anxiety* (New York: Vintage/Random
House, 2005), 8–9.

3. 2 Corinthians 5:16–17 NIV.

4. Zadie Smith, *White Teeth* (New York: Vintage/Random House,
2001), 49.

5. John Powell, *Why Am I Afraid to Tell You Who I Am? Insights
Into Personal Growth*, 2nd edition (Thomas More Association,
December 1995), XX.

6. I (Jon) once had a girl in college ask me how long it took me
to learn to speak English so I could come to college in the
United States. I told her around twenty years. She was blown
away and replied, "You must have really wanted to come
here." Cliché.

7. Pete Rollins gave a talk in our church basement that, though
controversial, is still one of the best things I have ever heard on
biblical community.

8. Romans 15:7 NIV.

9. Skye Jethani, *The Divine Commodity: Discovering a Faith Beyond Consumer Christianity* (Grand Rapids: Zondervan, 2009), 154.

10. Ephesians 4:2; John 13:34.

Chapter Nine

1. Psalm 33:5 NIV.

2. Psalm 97:2 NIV.

3. Psalm 103:6 NIV.

4. Amos 5:24 NIV.

5. Matthew 6:33 NIV.

6. 2 Corinthians 5:21 NIV.

7. 1 Peter 2:24 NIV 1984.

8. Major Campbell Roberts, from the 2006 Coutts Memorial Lecture at the Salvation Army College of Further Education in Sydney, Australia, part 4 of 5 on the centrality of biblical justice. http://salvos.org.au/edify/about-edify/what-is-biblical-justice/biblical-justice-has-a-partiality-to-it/ (accessed February 13, 2011).

9. Psalms 82:3–4 NLT.

10. Gary Haugen, *Good News About Injustice: A Witness of Courage in a Hurting World* (Downers Grove, IL: IVP, 2009), 94–96.

11. Statistics found at http://www.globalissues.org/article/26/poverty-facts-and-stats#src1 (accessed February 13, 2011).

12. Statistics found at http://www.avert.org/worldstats.htm (accessed February 13, 2011).

13. Statistics found at http://www.worldwatercouncil.org/index.php?id=23 (accessed February 13, 2011).

14. Matthew 6:9–10 TNIV.

15. Darren heard Gary Haugen say this during a message he was giving.

16. Philippians 2:5–8 NIV.

17. *The Collected Works of St. Teresa of Avila*, Vol. 1, ed. Otilio Rodriguez and Kieran Kavanaugh, IcsPubns (July 1, 1976).

Chapter Ten

Epigraphs—Albert Camus: Dictionary.com, *Columbia World of Quotations*, Columbia University Press, 1996. http://quotes. dictionary.com/the_modern_mind_is_in_complete_ disarray_knowledge (accessed: February 13, 2011); The apostle Paul: Romans 15:13 NIV.

1. Douglas Coupland, *Life After God* (New York: Pocket Books, 1994), the chapter called "little creatures."

2. John 19:25.

3. Luke 24:17–21 NIV.

4. 1 Maccabees 3:58–60.

5. Luke 24:19–21 NIV.

6. Luke 24:26–27 NIV.

Epilogue

1. Paul R. Dienstberger, *The America Republic: A Nation of Christians*, 2000. http://www.prdienstberger.com/nation/Chap6ndp.htm

2. Paul R. Dienstberger, *The America Republic: A Nation of Christians*, © 2000. http://www.prdienstberger.com/nation/ Chap6ndp.htm.

6. Habakkuk 3:2 TNIV.

READING GROUP GUIDE

CHAPTER 1

1. After years of "throwing herself into the Christian subculture and trying to grow spiritually," Catherine began to feel disillusioned. In a phrase, she was "bored, uninspired, and disappointed with her faith experience." We might call it burnout. Have you ever felt this way? What do you think has led to your feeling "burned-out"? Have you prayed about it? From whom, if anyone, have you sought counsel? What could you do to get motivated? Could you, in fact, do anything, or would any remotivating have to come from God?

2. When Catherine returned to the U.S. after a life-changing mission trip, she started a new ministry: working professionally in a strip club, applying the women's makeup before they went onstage. Rebecca, a onetime stripper, we learn, was converted through Catherine's witness. Yet for a time, Catherine was actually giving these women some of the

tools to better practice their "trade." This brings up serious questions. Should God's people go into the "cesspools" of the world in order to save souls? Should they ever contribute to someone's ability to sin in an effort to bring him or her to Christ? In other words, do the ends justify the means? Would Rebecca have gotten saved anyway?

3. The authors tell us that, while Christianity is growing in places like China, India, and South America, this is not the case in the United States. In fact, they say, "'nonreligious' has become the fastest-growing religious category." Why do you think this is? What started the West on its "fade to black" trajectory? What factors have contributed to America's—and the church's—continued drift away from God?

4. Darren and Jon compare the decline of Western Christianity to that scene in *Titanic* where the string quartet continues to play their instruments even as the ship sinks, pretending not to notice the ship is going down. Do you think the church is merely pretending that their "ship" is going down, or is she just plain unaware?

CHAPTER 2

1. Darren asks some soul-searching questions on pages 12 and 13, all of which bear reflection: Here's one: If God were a cosmic genie, and you could ask Him for anything, what would you ask for?

2. "For the most part," we read, "the desires and dreams of Christians are the same as non-Christians'. Essentially we are dreaming and longing for the same things . . . Maybe we're in worse shape than we thought." *Should* Christians want the same things that the world does, or, as Darren asks, "shouldn't out dreams be fueled by a different story?"? What should we wish for? Read Colossians 3:1–2 and Matthew 6:19–21. How do these verses speak to this question?

3. Read the quotes from *Culture Jam* on page 14. Thinking of your own day-to-day life, do you live a "designer" life as described by Lasn? How many "free, spontaneous minutes" do you have in the cycle Lasn depicted? Are your dreams in keeping with those of the "bulk of our population"?

4. Darren summarizes his apple-picking story by saying, "All too often we turn down the infinitely valuable in exchange for the trivial." Where can you find examples of this in twenty-first-century America? What valuable things are we exchanging for the "rotting apple"? What "rotting apples" do you find yourself running after?

CHAPTER 3

1. "As Western Christians we sometimes suffer from this 'silver medal syndrome,'" the authors write. "Though we have the highest standard of living in recorded history, we never quite seem to have enough." That brings to mind

the late Howard Hughes, one of the wealthiest men in the world in his day. When asked, "What would it take to make you happy?" his reply was, "Just a little bit more." Do you think the same way? In spite of anything you may have, do you always find yourself wanting more? How much would it take to satisfy you? How long would you be satisfied with that? Would you ever *truly* be satisfied? Why or why not?

2. In speaking of fashions and trends, the authors use the term "perceived obsolescence." When a new product, comes out, are you the first to buy it, or do you wait until some of the frenzy has died down—or forget it altogether? What if there's an upgrade? Take for instance the iPad. Every time there's a new "generation," do you just *have* to have it? What about clothing? Do you seem to be in a never-ending flurry of clothes replacement because something that was all the rage last year is no longer "in"? Or, like Jon's dad, do you do the "ugly stroll" from time to time (maybe even for a *looong* time)?

3. Reread the short section titled "A New Cultural Rhythm" on page 34. Is the cycle that Leonard presents consistent with your own life's "rhythm"? How much time do you spend enjoying your family as compared to sitting in front of the TV? Do you spend more time at the mall, ogling the latest designs and gadgets, than you do getting "physical" outdoors or at the gym? Are you having to work longer and harder than ever to pay for the things you've acquired? How can you change your rhythm? Would it take a couple of baby steps, or a radical shift in your thinking and your activities?

4. What do the authors say is the *first* thing one should do to break the cycle of greed and take hold of real life? (See page 35.) Do you agree? What stands in the way of your taking that step?

5. Do you ever catch yourself "calculating the cost-to-benefit ratio" of your friendships? (Be honest.) In which relationships do you feel you're being shortchanged? Are there others in which you're getting much more than you're "putting in"? Is this deliberate? Would you categorize yourself as more of a giver than a taker? If you're a taker, are you willing to put the "balance sheet" away and start giving without seeking to get?

CHAPTER 4

1. In the quote at the beginning of the chapter, Richard Rohr says, "Have you been loved well by someone? So well that you feel confident that person will receive you and will forgive your worst crime? That's the kind of security the soul receives from God." But the question is, do you *feel* that you have that kind of security? Are you confident—every day—that there's no sin that would take you "too far" for God's forgiveness? Or are there times when you feel you've crossed a line and God couldn't *possibly* have any more grace for you? What scriptures counter that myth?

2. Jon confesses that after he and Darren came to America, both filled with passion for God and for the lost, it wasn't long until "somehow the pressures and stress and distraction and struggles and planning and cares and critics had slowly won us over. . . . We'd lost the passion for Jesus."

Where are you on the passion index these days? Do you have the same fire and zeal you once had, or have the busyness and care of the American lifestyle begun to affect your passion for Christ? Has your loss of passion affected your church attendance? your availability for ministry involvement? your devotional time?

3. Sometimes the opposite can happen. Rather than stepping back from Christian service, you can become like the Ephesian church: heavy on "deeds," "more industrious than ever," and even mildly evangelistic—but doing it all out of a sense of *duty* rather than a passion for Christ. Is that you? Have you lost your first love? Can you echo the sentiment of the writer who said, "I felt like I was an infomercial for God—and I didn't even use the product"? What does it take to remain passionately in love with Jesus? To keep an individual and a community of believers filled with the love and *life* of God?

4. Is your pastor a "SuperPastor"? If so, are you counting on him (or her) to keep you inspired? What would happen if, perhaps because of his own personal struggles or a "dry" season in his life, his preaching suddenly no longer got you "fired up"? Would you—and maybe the rest of the congregation too—start looking for another SuperPastor? another church?

CHAPTER 5

1. Reflect for a moment on Billy Graham's response in the interview at the beginning of the chapter. Do you agree with his response? Is it right to strongly support an individual who has fallen into sin and disgrace, or should we distance ourselves from such a person until he or she "gets it right"? What's the reasoning behind your choice? Can you scripturally support your response?

2. Jon says that he was taken aback when a coworker told him, "You must hate me now that you know I'm gay . . . because you're a Christian, and all Christians hate gay people." Do you know someone who is gay who has that same impression? Do *you* give off that impression? What about your church? If a gay individual attended a service, would he feel a hatred toward himself, his sin, both, or neither? How should the church respond to gays who enter their congregations? to adulterers? to drug addicts? How did Jesus treat people who struggled with sin?

3. The fact is, we all struggle with sin. As the authors wrote, "Our sinful nature isn't an occasional temptation; it's the defining influence in our lives." They go on, then, on page 70, to list four examples. Using their same format, name your primary struggle (hint: there's probably more than one):

I crave _____, so I _____
_____.

4. C. S. Lewis once said that no one knows how bad he is until he has tried very hard to be good. When has that proved true for you? What did you try so hard to do—or not do— only to discover how "bad" you really are? Why couldn't you control your behavior? What should you do now?

5. Jon's story of "Pooooooh!" is a brilliant analogy of sin and the convicted (or self-condemned) sinner's reaction. When have you had an "accident" and then tried to clean it up yourself? What was the result? Were you successful, or did your efforts only make the mess bigger *and* set you up for a greater moral failure? What would you do differently now during the same struggle?

CHAPTER 6

1. Simon's story in the opening of the chapter is a sad example of a child who has suffered one of the worst kinds of betrayal. Has anyone betrayed you, as did Simon's parents, in the same or a similar way? Were you abandoned? molested? abused? What has been your response to your betrayers? Have you forgiven them? *Can* you? If you can't, do you even want to try, or, like Jonah, are you waiting with bated breath for your offenders to "gets theirs"?

2. Revisit the section titled "A Special Kind of Brutality," which discusses both the Assyrians' atrocities and Hitlers'. Now

think about some events that have taken place over the last decade, specifically, the assassinations of Saddam Hussein and Osama bin Laden. Do you feel any sadness that these individuals died without God? Do you wish they could have a second chance, or do you hope they're burning in hell? Thinking now of still-living terrorists, do you pray that they will come to the light of Christ, or do you hope that someone just blows them up? In other words, do you want *grace* for them, or *judgment*? Would you feel differently if someone you know and love were involved in their "cause"?

3. What if, instead Jesus' grace, He gave you what you really deserve for your sins? What punishment do you *feel* you deserve, based on the severity and number of your sins? What do you *really* deserve? Is it any less than what a mass murderer, a child rapist, or a world terrorist deserves? Does the size or degree of the sin matter to God, or is sin, sin? Does it take more grace for a big sin than a small one?

4. In this chapter, we read about the slayings of five Amish children, then the subsequent suicide of their killer. What do you think about the community attending the shooter's funeral? Was that really necessary? Do you think God required it, or should those affected just have stayed home and tended to their own emotional wounds? Could you have practiced "Amish forgiveness" if your loved one had been killed that day, or would you have hated the slayer? What do you think of the victims' parents' decision to financially support the gunman's family?

5. Have you recently forgiven someone who has done "immense hurt" to you? Should you also seek to reconcile with this offender, or, for wisdom's or safety's sake, should you draw the line at forgiveness? If you're uncertain, have you sought counsel to help you determine what's in your best interests? (You should.)

CHAPTER 7

1. Read the demon Screwtape's advice to Wormwood in the epigraph at the beginning of the chapter. Are you currently looking for a new church? Why? Was there a legitimate reason for leaving your former church, or—be honest here—are you just "church shopping," on the hunt for "the perfect church"? Can an individual find the "perfect church" for him or her? If so, will it stay perfect? If so, for how long? If not, why? What could make the perfect church sink into "imperfection"?

2. How would it impact the church if, rather than complaining about the style or volume of the worship music, we'd stop and remember that worship is not about (or for) us—it's for God? Would it change your own enthusiasm if, even when the songs are not to your liking, you remembered that they were written as praise to God? Have you ever found yourself worshipping wholeheartedly even when you didn't like the song or the musical style? What enabled you to engage in enthusiastic worship, even if you were "getting

nothing out of it" personally? If that has never happened, are you willing to lay aside your own musical preferences to worship God with abandon?

3. Time for more honesty. Do you tend to go to church to "get" or to "give"? If you find that you go to church most often to *receive*, what do you expect from your preacher, worship leader, or choir? To what do you contribute this expectation? If you go to *give*, what do you add to the service? To whom do you offer it?

4. Reflect on some of the movies and television shows named in this chapter. Do you find yourself buying into some of the lies generated by these films? Which ones? Does your lifestyle, dress, or conduct in any way reflect a belief in "the story we've been sold"? What do you do that is—beyond a doubt—informed by something or someone you've watched on TV or on the big screen? If so, what character do you admire? In what ways do you try to emulate him or her?

5. In this chapter, the authors state that "we cannot live independently of other believers and only think of our own needs. We become a part of a body, the family." Furthermore, Paul said that "no individual brick is big enough to contain the presence of God. It's all of us coming together . . . that creates a community big enough for God to truly be present in." Based on this text—and any other reasoning you might come up with on your own—what would you say to the person who tells you, "Oh, I don't *have* to go to church to be a Christian"?

CHAPTER 8

1. What efforts do you make to be accepted or to gain the approval of others? To what lengths have you gone to avoid rejection? Have you ever gone to *ridiculous* lengths? How ridiculous? To what lengths are you going *right now* to get attention or to impress someone? Are any of these efforts to gain—or keep—*God's* love or forgiveness?

2. If you have a Facebook, or other social network account, do you occasionally (or more than occasionally) post exaggerated—or downright false—information on your profile in order to reveal a side of you that doesn't exist (e.g., including an interest in "indie music and film so that we appear to have a unique and artsy side"). If so, why do you do this? Would the outcome be as pivotal as you think if you edited your page to project "you and only you"? What "friends" would you lose if you did?

3. Is there a sin in your life that you've been keeping to yourself—but shouldn't? If so, what would happen if you suddenly blurted it out in the middle of a small-group meeting or Sunday school class the way the cheating husband did in this chapter? Do you think you'd receive love and acceptance, or rejection and condemnation from your spiritual community? Would you feel relief at finally "getting it all out," or do you fear that your revelation would open up a can of worms that would lead to great personal loss, isolation, and even denunciation by those to whom you confessed?

CHAPTER 9

1. Are you preaching the gospel, or living the gospel, or both? What's the difference? Do you agree with Darren's initial assessment of the Christian singer who is trying to "live the gospel" without preaching it? Do you feel that she was "losing her way"? Can a person do one (preach versus live the gospel, or vice versa) at the expense of the other? If it's necessary to do both, is one more important than the other? Which one? How are you "living" the gospel?

2. What effect did reading global poverty, HIV, and child mortality numbers have on you? When you hear or read about the world's many overwhelming crises, which of these best describes your response?

   a. I send money to help out.

   b. I pray more and harder about the situation.

   c. I find a way to get physically involved in relief efforts.

   d. I don't do anything, because the problem is just too big to fix.

   Are you satisfied with your response? Do you think God is? If not, what changes can you make that will please God?

3. Who do you allow in your mental "greenroom"? Who do you—intentionally or unintentionally—exclude? From whose greenroom have *you* been or are you being excluded? How

did/does it make you feel? Who might you be willing to let in now? Whom did Jesus let in, even though he was harshly judged for it?

4. In this chapter, the authors introduced us to Willow Creek's "C.A.R.S." program, which reached out to women who had suffered from the "domino effect" and helped them in a tangible way. Who in your community is suffering? What could your church do to tangibly help these people? Have you suggested it to the leaders or your church, or would you be willing to? What if you were asked to spearhead the effort?

CHAPTER 10

1. Most Christians have heard an abundance of sermons peppered with the promises of Christ. But have those promises (e.g., Mark 11:23–24) "panned out" for you, personally? Or, as the authors wrote, could it be that "your marriage is a disappointment . . . your ministry has been a failure . . . a loved one has died . . . your child is far from God . . . [or] you are wrestling with a major illness"? If so, are you disappointed with Jesus, or, like the children of Israel, are you "tenaciously clinging" to your hope in Him, refusing to be dissuaded? If you've lost your faith, what would it take to turn your despair into renewed hope?

2. In the story of Josh and his battle with pornography, Lynne became a beacon of light, love, and hope to someone who had fallen, lost it all, and just about given up. Who do you know who has fallen into sin and been subsequently rejected, perhaps by your entire church? Did you contribute to that person's pain? Whether or not you did, what could you do *today* to breathe new life into that person's situation and restore the hope that has been lost? Are you willing to step out in faith?

EPILOGUE

1. After sharing some of America's "history of the unmistakable activity of God," the authors tell us that "in other parts of the world, God is moving in breathtaking power." We have already established that this is not the case in the U.S. What would bring the move and presence of God back to our nation so that we could once more experience the kind of movement witnessed in the 1850s? Is the ball in our court, or God's? If ours, then what would we need to do to experience a "fresh work of God" in our midst?

Stop living *over*, *under*, *from*, and *for* God and start living in communion *with* him.

ISBN: 9781595553799